THE IMPACT OF COVID-19 ON TEACHING AND LEARNING IN HIGHER EDUCATION

EDUCATION IN A COMPETITIVE AND GLOBALIZING WORLD

Additional books and e-books in this series can be found on Nova's website under the Series tab.

EDUCATION IN A COMPETITIVE AND GLOBALIZING WORLD

THE IMPACT OF COVID-19 ON TEACHING AND LEARNING IN HIGHER EDUCATION

SYLVIE STUDENTE, PhD
STEPHEN ELLIS, PhD
AND
BHAVINI DESAI, PhD
EDITORS

nova
science publishers
New York

NOTICE TO THE READER

Library of Congress Cataloging-in-Publication Data

ISBN: 978-1-53619-947-5

Published by Nova Science Publishers, Inc. † New York

CONTENTS

Preface   vii
    Sylvie Studente

Chapter 1   Enabling Transition to Online Teaching
    during COVID-19 through a Peer-Supported
    Collaborative Environment   1
    Bowen Yang, Zainurul Abd Rahman,
    Joannette J. (Annette) Bos and David Robertson

Chapter 2   Towards a Digital Pedagogy
    of Inclusive Active Distance Learning   23
    Helen Caldwell, Emma Whewell,
    Cristina Devecchi, Mary Quirke
    and Conor McGukin

Chapter 3   Staying Connected: Minimizing Isolation
    and Building Learning Communities
    via Chatbot Technology   51
    Sylvie Studente

Chapter 4   Designing and Delivering Online Education:
    One Size Does Not Fit All   77
    Filia Garivaldis, Mark Boulet,
    Bowen Yang and Sarah Kneebone

Chapter 5   The Effect of Mitigation Strategies on University
Student's Mental Health and Well Being:
A Review of Preliminary Studies   95
Sylvie Studente, Stephen Ellis and Bhavini Desai

Chapter 6   Wellbeing in the Time of COVID   111
*Stephen McKenzie, Michelle I Jongenelis
and Litza Kiropoulos*

Chapter 7   Examination of the Future for Lectures
and Seminars for Students -
in Business Modules, in the 21st Century   133
Philip Mayer

Chapter 8   How Has COVID-19 Shifted How We Support,
Recognise and Measure Student Engagement?   151
Rachel C. Bassett-Dubsky

Chapter 9   The Impact of COVID-19
on Student Engagement and Experience   175
Bhavini Desai

Chapter 10 Summing Up the Impact of COVID-19
on Student Experience and Expectations   193
Stephen Ellis

About the Editors   209

Index   213

PREFACE

Sylvie Studente[*], PhD

Regent's University London, London, United Kingdom

The outbreak of the COVID-19 pandemic has generated much uncertainty around the HE landscape. On the 20th March 2020 global lockdown measures were introduced which affected students in 142 countries worldwide (Karalis & Raikou, 2020). The outbreak led to university campuses closing and moving to an online mode for teaching and learning immediately (Masri & Sabzalieva, 2020; Bisht *et al*, 2020). Students have had to undertake self-directed learning as universities have had to close their classroom-doors (Mishra *et al*, 2020; Zhu & Liu, 2020). Numerous studies have reported that the physical closure of HE institutions has been detrimental to student learning worldwide (Jegede, 2020), whilst others have advocated the possible opportunities that may arise from reshaping HE through technologies (Sa & Serpa, 2020).

The disruption caused to education by the pandemic has had a significant impact on the learning experience for students (Hill & Fitzgerald, 2020). Student engagement with studies, with their lecturers and with other students is reported to be associated with successful learning (Zepke &

[*] Corresponding Author's E-mail: sylvie.studente@regents.ac.uk.

Leach, 2010; Docherty *et al,* 2018). Such interactions and engagement have been impeded by the move to full online-delivery of teaching and learning (Hill & Fitzgerald, 2020). When students are not engaged, this can be detrimental to their learning success and lead to feelings of disconnect (Bryson, 2014). The impact of the pandemic has had far reaching implications overall for teaching and learning in Higher Education; educators have reported that due to the immediate urgency of the lockdown there was little time to plan in advance for online delivery and assessment (Garcia-Penalvo *et al,* 2020). From a student perspective, self-directed study time has increased (Aucejo *et al,* 2020), levels of stress and anxiety experienced by students has increased (Karalis & Raikou, 2020; Baloran, 2020), and the lack of face-to-face interaction with lecturers and other students has led to feelings of isolation (Muhammad & Kainat, 2020).

From a financial perspective, the effects of the pandemic led to a loss for UK universities of £790 million during 2020 (Burki, 2020), which is forecast to increase to a loss of £2.6bn during 2021 Deloitte (2020). Enrolment numbers have declined, and the recruitment of international students, whom make up a high number of the market sector has been severely impacted. It is clear that HE institutions as a whole are facing significant challenges in these uncertain times. The situation faced by the pandemic highlights the need for Higher Education Institutions to grow more proactive to the needs of students beyond traditional classroom settings (Toquero, 2020).

This edited book addresses the need to examine the far-reaching impacts of the COVID-19 pandemic upon teaching and learning in Higher Education, and will report upon the challenges and opportunities associated with the impact of the pandemic, outlining current perspectives, practices and innovations which will contribute to an understanding of the current situation for Higher Education institutions. Research and best practices on adapting to online-modes of delivery and the implications of this will be shared. The need for this edited collection is to disseminate best practices with educators during this time of uncertainty.

This book is organised into three pertinent themes; innovation through technology, education and well-being, and student engagement and expectations. The first four chapters focus upon innovations through technology in the shift to online modes of delivery during the pandemic.

Chapter 1 – Restrictions imposed upon universities as a consequence of the COVID-19 pandemic led to universities moving towards a fully online model of teaching and learning. The required turn around for this was instant, and a number of challenges faced in terms of support, resources and technical skills for teaching staff. As a response to the needs of supporting educators during the transition, this chapter discusses the establishment of Teaching Online Meetups (TOMS) — a series of regular online sessions attended by academic and professional staff at the Monash Sustainable Development Institute at Monash University, Australia. This chapter provides insight on the critical role TOMS played in supporting staff in transitioning to online teaching during lockdown, and the building of the TOM community which enabled sharing of online teaching practices. The community was used to not only share online teaching practices, but also for testing online teaching tools and providing hands-on experience with online technologies in live group settings. The chapter provides an evaluation of how the approach assisted staff with developing digital capabilities, and capacity to gain confidence in online teaching.

Chapter 2 – This chapter discusses Active Distance Learning (ADL) and Universal Design for Learning (UDL) as pedagogical approaches to online learning. Within the chapter, the authors demonstrate how the UDL framework can be used alongside ADL to enhance online inclusivity. The concept is based on the idea of offering multiple opportunities for engagement, representation, action and expression in online learning environments, and providing choice in how learners access information and display their learning. ADL extends upon a number of techniques such as; flipped learning, MOOCs, gaming and learning management systems in offering asynchronous and synchronous opportunities for learner generated content creation via online learning tools. Digital tools effectively facilitate sharing, and the cyclical making and talking, posting and responding that takes place synchronously and asynchronously within online communities can positively enhance learning. Digital posts and artefacts can act as stepping stones for re-discussion, re-making and re-mixing content. ADL is an approach to the design of online learning that has been explored across a number of online education courses at the University of Northampton, including the online MA Education, and was extended across other courses when on campus teaching was suspended due to COVID-19. This chapter discusses the concept of Active Distance Learning as a pedagogical approach to designing and teaching in remote learning settings, providing examples of digital pedagogies and tools in action.

Chapter 3 – Due to the physical closure of universities owing to the pandemic, there has been an increase in demand for new approaches towards e-learning. The lack of face-to-face interaction with lecturers and other students has led to feelings of isolation for some students. It is at a time now more than ever that reliance on technology for social interaction is of utmost importance. Another detrimental impact owing to the physical closure of university campuses has been that of student engagement. When students are not engaged, this can be detrimental to their learning success and lead to further feelings of disconnect. Feelings of "social isolation" are reported to be a key cause of low engagement for international students. These feelings can be exacerbated if students receive little opportunity to engage in learning communities to receive peer support. This chapter reports upon two studies introducing chatbot technology to develop learning communities at a London University, with a largely international student base. The first study, a pilot, was conducted over the autumn term of 2019, and the focus was twofold; to ease the transition for students into their first year of university study, and to increase study engagement. The second study was carried out during the lockdown of 2020 and focussed upon modules in which previous engagement levels had been low. This chapter reports upon how the chatbot was implemented during lockdown to not only help students feel more connected, but also how the chatbot was incorporated within teaching and learning activities during online modes of delivery. It is emphasised that chatbots provide the opportunity to act as an *"intelligent bridge"* between technology and education. The benefits of which, can be garnered in instances where remote and/or blended learning scenarios are of paramount focus.

Chapter 4 – The differences between face to face and online modes of learning are many and diverse, and the majority of courses translated to online delivery adopt a process of retrofitting. This process involves adapting, top down, existing learning materials and resources to a new delivery mode. For some courses, this has meant developing pre-recorded lectures or delivering lectures in real-time through teleconferencing software, adding practice quizzes or discussion forums for students' self-paced asynchronous engagement, or replacing in-class group-based "butcher paper" activities with collaborative synchronous work using Google Docs/Slides. In any of these cases, the retrofitting process involves supplanting instructor-led learning with some student-centred activities through planned intercommunications, interactivity, and collaborations between learners. This chapter describes two behaviour change programs of study developed by BehaviourWorks Australia (BWA), a specialist behavioural science enterprise within the Monash Sustainable Development Institute (MSDI), and the efforts of BWA teaching staff to deliver these programs in the online mode in 2020. The first case study discusses the experience of translating an on-campus unit of study originally designed for face-to-face delivery, into the fully online mode in response to the Australian government's first imposed "lockdown" restrictions. The second case study discusses the building of a purposely designed fully online micro-credential. Reflections are shared on the key principles and priorities considered in developing and delivering these programs. Common themes across both case studies are discussed in terms of good practice in educational design, that apply irrespective of delivery mode. The second theme of this edited collection is that of; education and well-being which are addressed in chapters five, six and seven.

Chapter 5 – In response to the pandemic, universities closed their physical premises, suspended face-to-face teaching and moved to online modes of delivery. Despite the physical closure of campuses, universities have generally responded well in providing innovative teaching and learning online to continue providing education to students despite restrictions. However, although implementing online learning was necessary for students to continue with their studies, research reports both social and psychological impacts on students. While some students have responded to changes in educational strategies with resilience, others have reported detrimental impacts to their mental health. Overall increases in levels of anxiety and depression experienced by students have a number of consequences in terms of; academic performance and progression, struggling to focus on academic studies, and decreased motivation with studies. This is coupled with changes in social dimensions, and social restrictions are reported to lead to levels of elevated anxiety and symptoms of depression. This chapter provides a review on preliminary studies which highlight the urgent need for strategies to support student's metal health and wellbeing. As such, this chapter concludes with recommendations to assist in supporting students during these challenging times.

Chapter 6 – The University of Melbourne, Australia and its largest faculty; Medicine, Dentistry and Health Sciences (FMDHS) was faced with substantial challenges caused by the COVID-19 induced lockdown in 2020, which led to the sudden replacement of its traditional physical education capacities with online capacities. The University responded to the emerging known and unknown effects of this crisis by recognising the unmet psychological, social, emotional, and physical wellbeing needs of students, as well as recognising their academic success needs and the inter-relationship of these needs. In response to these needs, wellbeing-enhancing resources for staff, students, and health professionals were developed to assist people with responding optimally to their COVID-related wellbeing challenges. These challenges included staff and students' sudden isolation, and full immersion in online education, and also health professionals suddenly having to manage their own and their clients' isolation and other psychological and physical health challenges. This chapter describes The University of Melbourne's development and implementation of three innovative and potentially transferable online education COVID responses: 1. A student wellbeing and success orientation module, 2. A series of free short online courses for health professionals, and 3. A series of free short online courses for students. These offerings successfully met temporary and ongoing needs for large scale wellbeing, success, and health-enhancing online education resources. This chapter describes each of these online education resources, and provides examples of implementation.

Chapter 7 – The prevalence and proliferation of online teaching owing to the COVID-19 pandemic has hastened the used of modern technology for seminars and lectures. This chapter addresses the value and usefulness of lectures and seminars in higher education, and presents a discussion on relevant theories addressing lecturing and course design. The third theme of this edited collection is that of; student engagement and expectations, which are addressed in final three chapters.

Chapter 8 – HE educators have seen both improvements and additional barriers to student engagement during COVID-19. Attendance in particular, seems to have been a measure less fit for purpose, being both improved (in that students are present/logging in) but less meaningful (in that attendance is not leading to work completion or interaction). It is important to recognise the benefits and opportunities of digitally enabled practice whilst also staying aware that digital exclusion remains an issue. This chapter addresses the impact of COVID-19 upon the perceptions of student engagement, and reports upon the progression of a level 4 cohort at an East England University. Specifically, this chapter addresses measurements of "engagement", and explores engagement, achievement and progression in collaboration with the student cohort. Recommendations are drawn that Higher Education institutions should retain the inclusive flexibilities of lockdown learning moving forward.

Chapter 9 – The impact of the pandemic has had far reaching implications overall for teaching and learning in Higher Education, where educators have reported that due to the immediate urgency of the lockdown there was little time to plan in advance for online delivery and assessment. In the short term, institutions implemented immediate measures to support students and education systems in coping with the disruptions and impact of school and university closures. The disruption caused to education by the pandemic has had a significant impact on the learning experience for students, especially International students who had to decide whether to return home with limited information about when they might return, or remain in their host country with restricted employment and education opportunities. This in-turn affected student's expectations from their academic institutions, their engagement with their tutors and peers and most importantly, severely altered their experiences. In response to the need for providing a seamless learning experience, and to support tutors during this transition, in March 2020, a cross-institutional approach at Regents University London (RUL) led to the establishment of the RADAR framework. The acronym RADAR refers to five broad learning activities: Research, Acquire, Discuss, Action, Reflect. In developing the RADAR framework, attention was turned to how this could work for all modules in a remote setting. The intention of the framework was to work towards fulfilling expectations by providing a more engaging experience. This chapter discusses the struggles of adjusting to moving education online, followed by a discussion on understanding student engagement and expectations. The RADAR development and steps involved is outlined and how this affected the delivery, assessment and engagement within modules.

Chapter 10 - The shock of COVID has changed the HE landscape. Amongst the many questions that the public health crisis of 2020/21 has forced the higher education (HE) sector to confront is that of the student experience. UK HE real student retention rates are typically around the 70-75% mark, meaning that many students drop out before completing their studies for whatever reason. Or they may have been wrongly recruited in the first place. Expectations not being met is one of the causes of drop out and many institutions have increased their attention to this area through resourcing greater student support, for example by making counselling and mental health interventions more widely accessible. Demand for student support services however is rising to help meet ever increasing student expectations, but the picture could get much worse as worrying concerns over student wellbeing and inclusivity are now becoming heard ever more loudly. This chapter embraces the key themes from the previous sections of this book, looking more closely at the student experience and concludes with suggested steps to be actioned with regard to the student experience and expectations.

REFERENCES

Aucejo, E., French, J., Paola, M., Araya, U. & Zafar, B. (2020). The impact of COVID-19 on student experiences and expectations: Evidence from a survey. *Journal of Public Economic.* 191. Doi: 104271

Baloran, E. (2020). Knowledge, attitudes, anxiety and coping strategies of students during COVID-19 pandemic. *Journal of Loss and Trauma.* 25, 8. Pp 635 – 642.

Bisht, R., Jasola, S. & Bisht, I. (2020). Acceptability and challenges of online higher education in the era of COVID-19: a study of student's perspective. *Asian Education and Development Studies.* Doi: https://doi.org/10.1108/AEDS-05-2020-0119

Bryson, C. (2014). *Understanding and Developing Student Engagement.* Routledge.

Burki, T. (2020). COVID-19: Consequences for higher education. *The Lancet.* 2, 6. Pp 758.

Deloitte. (2020). *COVID-19 and Impacts on the Higher Education Sector: Building Reslience.* [online]. Available from: https://www2.deloitte.com/uk/en/pages/public-sector/articles/COVID-19-and-impacts-on-the-higher-education-sector.html

Docherty, A., Warkentin, P., Borgen, J., Garthe, K., Fischer, K. & Najjar, R. (2018). Enhancing student engagement: innovative strategies for intentional learning. *Journal of Professional Nursing.* 34, 6. Pp 470 - 474

Garcia-Penalvo, F., Corell, A., Abella-Garcia, V. & Grande-De-Prado, M. (2020). Recommendations for mandatory online assessment in higher education during the COVID-19 pandemic. In Burgo, D, Tlili, A & Tabacoo, A (Eds.) *Radical Solutions for Education in a Crisis Context.* Springer.

Hill, K. & Fitzgerald, R. (2020). Student perspectives of the impact of COVID-19 on learning. *All Ireland Journal of Higher Education.* 12, 2. Pp 1 – 9.

Sylvie Studente

Karalis, T. & Raikou, N. (2020). Teaching at the times of COVID-19: Inferences and implications for higher education pedagogy. *International Journal of Academic Research in Business and Social Sciences.* 10, 5. Pp 479 – 493.

Masri, A. & Sabzalieva, E. (2020). Dealing with disruption, rethinking recovery: policy responses to the COVID-19 pandemic in Higher Education. *Policy Design and Practice.* 3, 3. Pp 312 – 333.

Muhammad, A. & Kainat, A. (2020). Online learning amid the COVID-19 pandemic: student's perspectives. *Journal of Pedagogical Sociology and Psychology.* 2, 1. Pp 45 – 51.

Sa, M. & Serpa, S. (2020). The COVID-19 pandemic as an opportunity to foster the sustainable development of teaching in higher education. *Sustainability.* 12, 20. Pp 8525.

Toquero, C. (2020). Challenges and opportunities for higher education amid the COVID-19 pandemic: The Philippine context. *Pedagogical Research.* 5, 4. Doi: https://doi.org/10.29333/pr/7947

Zepke, N. & Leach, L. (2010). Improving student engagement: ten proposals for action. *Active Learning in Higher Education.* 11, 3. Pp 167 – 177.

In: The Impact of COVID-19 on Teaching ...   ISBN: 978-1-53619-947-5
Editors: S. Studente, S. Ellis et al.   © 2021 Nova Science Publishers, Inc.

Chapter 1

ENABLING TRANSITION TO ONLINE TEACHING DURING COVID-19 THROUGH A PEER-SUPPORTED COLLABORATIVE ENVIRONMENT

Bowen Yang[*], *Zainurul Abd Rahman,*
Joannette J. (Annette) Bos and David Robertson
Monash Sustainable Development Institute,
Monash University, Australia

ABSTRACT

At the start of 2020, COVID-19 restrictions have led universities to move most face-to-face teaching to online. Across the sector, traditional university teaching staff were faced with a common challenge: adapting classroom teaching to online in a short window of time. The difficulty of this transition was often compounded by limited support, resources, technical skills and knowledge required to create socially-engaged online classroom experiences that supported learning as effectively as their face-to-face teaching.

---

[*] Corresponding Author's E-mail: Bowen.yang@monash.edu.

As a response to the needs of supporting educators during the transition, in March 2020, a cross-institute approach at the Monash Sustainable Development Institute (MSDI), Monash University Australia led to the establishment of the Teaching Online Meetups (TOM) — a series of regular online sessions attended by academic and professional staff in the Institute. The initiative gained momentum across 2020, and later expanded to include across other faculties of Monash University.

In this chapter, we firstly discuss the critical roles TOM played in supporting staff's successful transitioning into online teaching during the lockdown and outline the process involved in the establishment and operation of TOM, including the management of TOM's resource site. Next, we explain TOM's community building and staff capacity development approach, which centres around creating an open and safe space to share online teaching practices, test new online teaching tools and activities, and provide hands-on experience with online technologies in a live group setting. We evaluate how this practical approach helped staff to develop their digital capacity effectively and gain confidence in online teaching. Lastly, we discuss the pattern of technology adoption and the different levels of needs of participants. We reflect on how the progression of session topics has continued to address the community's online teaching needs. We conclude with recommendations for others in adopting similar approaches at an institutional level.

Keywords: peer support, capacity building, online teaching, transition

INTRODUCTION

Border closures and a series of lockdowns due to COVID-19 in 2020 left higher education institutions around the globe with one feasible option to deliver education — transitioning to fully online course delivery. From 13th March, the Australian State of Victoria began a full-scale lockdown. With the government restrictions in place, almost everything was advised, wherever possible, to shift to an online environment, including all teaching and learning activities that took place in universities. Across the sector, higher education teaching staff were faced with a common challenge: adapting face-to-face classroom teaching to fully online within a short period of time. At Monash University Australia, as with many other universities across the country, the need to swiftly transition to online teaching posed enormous challenges for educators as entering lockdown coincided with the start of the new teaching period. In the first few months, educators who were delivering their classes online scrambled to redevelop teaching plans, upskill in online teaching tools, and manage and meet student needs and expectations. For many, the key challenge was in the technical implementation of classroom activities and the confidence in the effective use of online technologies.

THE IMPACT ON STUDENT EXPERIENCE

On the receiving end of education, university students who started in the new semester were missing out on the whole-of-campus experience, especially the lecturer-student and students' peer interaction.

The lack of social interaction in the online environment was in contrast to a typical university experience — students attend classes not just to learn but to develop connections with their teachers and peers. It is well known that the social aspect of learning is crucial to students' overall educational experience (Hurst, Wallace, and Nixon 2013; Mucharraz and Venuti 2020). There are numerous studies pointing to a positive correlation between students' feeling of belonging to a course and the student outcomes. Positive outcomes are not restricted to academic achievements but increase the level of overall well-being, an aspect which was very important during COVID restrictions (Lapointe and Reisetter 2008; Thomas, Herbert and Teras 2014; Peacock and Cowan 2019; Murphy, Boucher and Logel, 2021). For some students, coming to online classes was their only opportunity to connect with other human beings.

Moreover, we discovered that online classrooms did not always provide equal opportunities for students to participate. A few vocal students tended to dominate discussions whereas the majority found it difficult to participate. Less confident students, especially international students, found it hardest to engage in online classes. Their situation was exacerbated by the fact that it is easier to "hide" online and accidently slip out of the educator's attention.

Our educators were aware of the need to create socially-engaged and participatory classroom experiences in an online environment. This, at times, placed extra pressure on educators who were not confident nor experienced in the design and delivery of online classes. Some common challenges voiced by educators include:

- Recreating face-to-face classroom learning activities in an online environment was not straightforward, and not everything worked during that translation.
- Dealing with teaching and solving technical issues at the same time was a struggle in a live class context.
- Many were forced to adopt a less effective "trial and error" approach instead of being able to access and deploy a best practice approach.
- Educators experienced difficulty engaging all students, especially international students.
- It was hard to understand and evaluate strengths of different online platforms and tools to make informed choices
- Integrating different digital tools in a seamless way posed many challenges
- The transition felt overwhelming and educators were not always willing or able to embrace the changes, and the additional work that came with it.

The multitude of challenges and the need for speedy solutions rendered conventional professional development and support methods impractical. Due to the speed of change, the broader University, like many businesses and organisations, was limited in the support they could provide to staff in this immediate transition. At the same time, the university's IT services who provide on-call technical assistance were overwhelmed by a surge of requests. Under the circumstance, an alternative approach that provided effective, timely and more personalised support to the education transition was imperative.

PEER SUPPORT

Peer support originated from physiology practices as a well-established clinical approach when it comes to facilitating recovery (Chamberlin 1998; Mead and MacNeil 2004; Wrobleski et al. 2015). In general terms, the notion of "peer support" derives from a situation where people who share common experiences or face similar challenges come together to offer support in any form, comfort, skills, knowledge that comes through experience (Riessman 1990). In the higher education environment, peer support is often reported as an alternative support for sustainable use of innovative teaching approaches (Topping 1996) and occurs when people provide knowledge, experience, emotional, social or practical help to each other. For several decades, peer support methods have been credited with a range of beneficial effects. Peer support has become a significant element for improved outcomes with hands-on applied solution-based approaches that engage people with different skills and knowledge to support similar needs of others (Peersman and Fletcher 2019). Peer support as an organised strategy for giving and receiving help can be understood as an extension of the natural human tendency to respond compassionately to shared difficulty (Penny 2018). Sometimes referred to as self-help or mutual aid, peer support has been used by people dealing with different types of social circumstances, emotional challenges, and health issues (Penney, Mead, and Prescott 2008). Peer support may be actioned in formal or informal environments, within one-on-on or in a group-based setting.

THE BEGINNING OF A PEER-SUPPORTED COLLABORATIVE ENVIRONMENT

The overnight shift of teaching mode plunged MSDI educators into the deep end: many felt that they had to deal with an emergency that they were not ready for. In response to the situation, a cross-institute approach initiated by the authors of this chapter with active, senior-level support promptly assessed the most critical needs within MSDI. Two areas for support were identified: firstly, to maintain the quality of education and teaching standards, educators needed to quickly adopt online teaching best practices, tools and technologies to engage students who transitioned to studying online; and secondly, to get started or to become more confident in online teaching, educators required live technical support in their online classrooms. The following two sections discuss a response to each area separately.

Adopting Online Teaching Best Practices, Tools and Technologies

In response to the first need, a group of MSDI academic and professional staff involved in online teaching started to self-organise informal online meetups to exchange ideas and share experiences about online teaching. Initially started without any fixed agenda, the meetups centred around forthcoming educators sharing recently-occurred classroom scenarios of "what worked" and "what didn't work" in their online classes, accompanied by personal reflections and group discussion around online teaching best practices. As the semester progressed, the group of around 15 participants decided to meet every two weeks to stay on top of important updates.

Alongside online meetings, participants frequently exchanged online resources via emails and a shared Google drive. With the widespread use of crowd-produced resources, many caution that educators may find themselves adrift in an ocean of information (Ferguson and Buckingham Shum 2012) with little guidance on how it works technically, and how to link it together synchronously (Paulin and Haythornthwaite 2016). Under the MSDI process, a master document containing an index of all resources was collectively compiled and regularly maintained. This bank of resources includes the latest teaching online strategies, class planning templates, getting-started guide with technologies, as well as re-usable materials for student induction on a specific online tool contributed by individual educators. Thanks to this collaborative process, educators had an up-to-date peer-curated and peer-generated repository at their disposal, instead of searching for and evaluating the relevance of resources individually. This process assembled a wealth of accessible and open-source teaching materials, crowdsourced by educators and practitioners who could prioritise sharing the most useful material for rapid improvement of online teaching practices.

Providing Online Live Support

Educators who sought live peer support were mainly in need of extra technical assistance using online video conferencing applications such as Zoom and Microsoft Teams in running live workshops. A lack of confidence in troubleshooting issues such as student login, audio connection, managing breakout rooms, and using collaborative online documents were affecting educators in effectively managing their online classes. Even experienced online educators encountered challenges in simultaneously teaching content and supporting students who struggled to adopt and effectively use digital learning tools.

Operated in a reciprocal and sometimes altruistic manner, educators who were confident with their technical capabilities or those who had experience running online workshops came forward to offer assistance to their colleagues. Depending on who they were helping with, the live support assistance ranged from co-hosting the online video conferencing application, providing rapid 1:1 support to address students' technical issues, to monitoring chat and facilitating breakout rooms, etc. The process of receiving peer support from colleagues not only increased educators' confidence level in leading their online classes in those peer-supported sessions but also created crucial opportunities where they observe and learn from how issues were dealt with by a more competent peer. For experienced online educators, peer support enabled them to test more ambitious or novel approaches with greater confidence when leading classes; and when supporting others, they were able to focus on, and better understand, the student experience, as they were alleviated of the responsibility for content delivery. At MSDI, educators were fortunate to have the in-house capacity to make this type of support available as the Institute was already preparing for some of our educational offerings to go online.

Two months after the inception of the meetups, it was evident that the practice-focused experience sharing in online meetups and a peer reviewed online repository provided a critical and timely capacity building mechanism to MSDI educators as evidenced by increased uptake of online teaching practices and tools. For those who were less confident in their technical skills, peer-based live classroom support served as a confidence booster in the early months of online teaching.

THE FORMALIZATION OF TEACHING ONLINE MEETUPS (TOM)

From April to July 2020, the peer-supported environment grew organically within the institute. Meanwhile, the administrative process became more established: every session was recorded with participant consent and the content documented in detailed meeting notes. A dedicated shared folder was created, allowing participants' easy access to session notes and recordings. Reminder emails were sent before and after the session. By August, the meetups reached a stage where the MSDI team realised that this initiative could offer broader benefit to the University.

Monash's Education Academy (MEA), a central university learning and teaching unit, supported the idea to extend this initiative to other Monash Faculties, as MEA recognised it as a valuable educator support approach which complements what they are doing in professional development. The MSDI team took onboard several suggestions made by MEA including focusing on promoting the online meetups — named as Teaching Online Meetups (TOM). Thanks to the central push through university newsletters and faculty word of month, the meetups were quickly gaining momentum; and the number of participants quadrupled by the end of 2020.

As TOM continued to expand, managing its core resources such as recordings, notes and activity repository in an online shared drive became ineffective. For one thing, the shared folder structure, though easy to set up, was increasingly difficult to navigate as more folders were added. For another, the lack of a graphic interface made the resources less appealing, especially for new participants.

To overcome these shortcomings, a new website was soft launched to TOM participants in August 2020. The website is based on Microsoft Sharepoint — a web-based collaborative platform with a university license. The platform enables secure access through the university's Single-Sign-On portal. The Sharepoint site, called Teaching Engaging Online Class (TEOC), is linked to TOM as a supplementary website, providing participants with easy access to TOM-related resources.

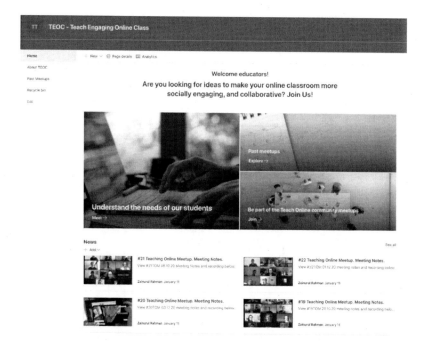

Figure 1. TEOC Sharepoint site homepage.

An innovative feature of the website content is the inclusion of templated online lesson plans co-developed by TOM participants. Inspired by public websites such as Hyper Island Toolbox and Playmeo, which feature re-usable teaching resources, these lesson plan templates prescribe a sequence of learning activities, validated by educators and categorised in terms of timing, purpose and minimal setup. For example, an 120-minute online workshop template encompasses a range of teaching purposes such as "Start a Class", "Present Content", "Get Students Talking", "Energiser", "Get Students Doing" and "End a Class". A possible activity is suggested for each purpose, giving educators a head start if they are to adopt these activities. The lesson plan also includes hyperlinks to activities that have been written out on a dedicated information page with technology requirements, step-by-step guide, variations and customisable slides (see Figure 2).

120 MINS LESSON PLAN

Timing	Purpose	Activity	Setup
10 mins	Start a Class	**Introduction and Settle the Room** The facilitator runs a simple 'pulse check' activity to focus the class's attention.	Everyone together
20 mins	Present Content	**Webinar** The educator presents a slide deck on the workshop content.	Everyone together Screen Sharing slides
20 mins	Get Students Talking	**Prompted Breakouts (Content)** The educator provides one or more discussion prompts based on the webinar and students move to breakouts to discuss these.	Breakouts of 3-4 people per group Educator moves around
5 mins	Stretch Break	**Video and Sound Off** (Optional: Play a 5-minute pop song)	
5 mins	Energiser	**Simon Says** Educator or appointed students lead the activity to get the students to move physically	Everyone Together Videos on
40 mins	Get Students Doing	**Collaborative Analysis** Students move into breakouts and work together on a task. They capture their results via a digital whiteboard tool.	Breakouts of 3-4 people per group Educator moves around
10 mins	Get Students Talking	**Prompted Breakouts (Content)** After completing their task, students reflect and discuss what they discovered and learned.	Breakouts of 3-4 people per group
10 mins	End a Class	**Learning Checkpoint** The educator closes the class by seeking questions and reinforcing key messages or outcomes.	Everyone together

Figure 2. A sample of a 120-minute lesson plan.

TOM'S APPROACH TO BUILDING EDUCATOR CONFIDENCE IN ONLINE TEACHING

As discussed in the MSDI student research earlier, the need for socially-engaged and interactive online classes place higher expectations on educators. What used to be "good to haves" are now "must haves" under the context of teaching in a period of lockdown where requirements on the quality of online tuition are becoming even more demanding (Gasevic 2020;

Mpofu 2020). To be a qualified online teacher, one is expected to assume multiple roles such as a content facilitator, an ICT user and a Learning Designer (Mallinson, Justine, and Krull 2015). In terms of facilitation skills, educators are expected to not only to facilitate the learners' growing understanding of course content, but to facilitate a range of online activities that are supportive of student learning (Goodyear et al. 2001; Wilson and Stacey 2004).

Our own understanding of the challenges and situations facing educators transitioning to online teaching, based on our day-to-day interaction with educators, tells us that a key aspect of developing skills and competencies as an online teacher is confidence building. It is about having the assurance of knowing that something will work in certain expected ways, be it a classroom activity or a piece of technology. In other words, confidence has to be built through validated experiences. In the early months of online meetups, it was discovered that participants found practice sharing and group testing of tools valuable. The experiential, practical, and hands-on aspects of the meetups and the way knowledge is shared in a peer-based environment are what set TOM apart from other types of formal training or capacity building programs provided by the university. Operated with a flexible, informal and open approach, the meetups were able to aptly respond to educators immediate teaching needs, through the following ways:

Peer-Supported Practice Sharing

The most valuable part of the meetups was opportunities to learn from peers about how they have successfully implemented an online teaching strategy or conducted a classroom activity. This often involved the educator who was sharing the practice simulating in real time with other participants who were treated as students. From a participant's perspective, the fact that they were not only able to watch the demonstration but to participate in an activity proved to be appealing and beneficial. Additionally, listening to colleagues from the same institution sharing a teaching practice offered them with an authentic context surrounding the practice.

For example, educators participating in the early meetups were interested in learning about how to conduct effective online icebreaker activities. They were curious to see how other colleagues have done it successfully with their students, and the strategies that they employed to overcome obstacles. A specific example of this was in the delivery of 'speed networking' via Zoom to give participants short, 1:1 interactions with peers at the start or end of a class, something noted by students as infrequent or missing in online delivery. This social icebreaker method was successful in testing within TOM, and was deployed by its creator as well as several TOM peers, in curricular learning contexts as well as professional meetings with work colleagues.

A more content-driven example of sharing resulting in peer adoption of a technique was when a participant gave a live demonstration of a simple, flexible, game-show style activity called "Who Wants To Be An Entrepreneur?". The format allowed the educator to introduce key concepts, each paired with a self-assessment question, for which students recorded their responses to build an overall score/profile. They then discussed their results with peers in a subsequent breakout. The live demonstration offered TOM participants immediate insight into the 'student' view - which was easy to understand and engaging - and also enabled the lead educator to articulate the transferability of the format and its functions. The approach was simple and effective enough that an MSDI TOM participant adapted it for use in a class just two days later, to good effect.

In terms of a general process, educators who were sharing a new activity would start by introducing the gist of the task, then running a miniature version of the activity using the same prompts that they had used in their classes. This context setting followed by an immediate experiential component made the shared practice tangible and relevant to other TOM participants, while the reflection and discussion of challenges implementing the practice provided participants with concrete strategies and useful insights to pick up and use what they had experienced.

Hands-On Testing with Online Tools

The second frequently requested feature of the meetups was about learning new or updated features of online tools. Similar to the sharing of teaching practices, the discussion around technology was always accompanied by hands-on experience with the tools through individual or collective testing. For example, when Zoom was examined in the first few meetups, participants frequently tested features such as the different formats of breakout rooms, screen annotation, polling and screen sharing by role playing a host, co-hosts and a participant so they were able to familiarise themselves with the different interfaces associated with respective roles. The approach to acquiring the know-how of a tool through hands-on testing with peers prompted individual educators to use TOM as a way to gain confidence before adopting the tools in the real class.

Personal Reflections and Group Discussions

The hands-on aspect as a main feature of the meetups was complemented by individual participants' personal reflections about their online teaching and learning experiences, as effective capacity building should provide not only authentic contexts but opportunities for participants to critically reflect on their learning as they progress through their journey (Wilson and Stacey 2004). These purposeful reflections usually sparked off further discussion on issues or topics that were methodological than technical. For example, questions were raised such as "what is the worst practice in online teaching?", "what are the effective ways to engage international students?"; or "which order should I follow in terms of technology adoption, from easy to advanced?". The reflective moments helped to build a sense of sharing understanding amongst participants who acquired a deepened understanding of the discourse around online education. It is important to highlight that many early reflections included frank assessments of classes and activities that had been difficult, or failed entirely. This honest and open sharing provided a sense of camaraderie and reduced the sense of pressure to be 'perfect' in delivery, which, in turn, fostered participants' confidence to keep trying new things.

An Open Space for Sharing

The effectiveness of the meetups depends, to a large extent, on how much participants want to engage and how willing they want to contribute. While confident and tech savvy educators are often willing to share without reservation, not everyone is on an equal footing. In fact, because transition occurred quickly, the majority of TOM participants perceived themselves lacking certain skills required for an online educator. To prompt equal participation, the meetups have been promoted as an experimental and non-judgemental space to try new ideas. Participants are encouraged to share anything that was considered of value worth sharing, from testing out an updated version of an "old" activity to just spending five minutes reflect on the challenges in last week's class. To give participants an easy time, slides were deemed optional and time flexible. In fact, some participants benefited from a quick demonstration of an activity that would not be considered substantial by a formal presentation standard. Through this bite-sized and micro-learning, participants were able to gain critical confidence in running the activity.

ADDRESSING DIFFERENT LEVELS OF NEEDS

In one of the most established social science theories, Rogers (2003) outlines five adopter categories when it comes to a new idea, behaviour or technology — innovators, early adopters, early majority, late majority and laggards. The term "diffusion of innovation" exhibits a bell-shaped distribution curve amongst the five categories. Over the course of TOM's running, we observed that participants were falling under a few of these categories — their perception and attitudes towards the transition to online teaching and their level of technical expertise were markedly different. We also observed different levels of anxiety associated with the use of new technology (Lock and Johnson 2016). For example, early adopters perceive the transition as a challenge that they needed to overcome and they achieved a sense of accomplishment by experimenting with new technologies and novel approaches to teaching. They become a role model for others, and act as a resource for other staff (Gurley et al. 2018). On the other hand, late majority or laggards were hesitant about change, though they also perceived that transition was imperative in order to accommodate the new format of delivery. They expressed more anxiety and placed a significant demand on classroom support. Similarly, with regard to educators' confidence of adopting different types of technology: innovators and early adopters were constantly seeking to identify new tools or trial novel approaches of integrating new tools to their teaching, whereas their less confident peers prone to be more risk averse — sticking to what they were already familiar with or waiting for an assurance that similar approaches have been adopted by their colleagues.

In the text below, we briefly discuss, in our experience with TOM to date, how the meetups benefited different types of participants — enthusiasts and techies who are willing to share, the majority who are happy just being a participant, and those who struggle and in need of support. We also reflect on how TOM continued to stay relevant by staying on top of the most urgent and important needs of its participants.

Peer Support is Beneficial to Different Types of Participants

The peer support environment of the online meetups operated primarily through voluntary sharing and testing of teaching practices. For early adopters, enthusiasts and competent educators, TOM provided important opportunities for them to showcase and validate their ideas with real participants before implementing them in the classroom. Furthermore, early adopters took advantage of the meetups to extend their horizontal networks, that is, their personal networks extend to interdisciplinary and cross-functional groups (Geoghegan 1995).

As for the early or late majority group, TOM provided much-needed capacity building opportunities, actualised through a non-conventional, flexible and collaborative peer-supported environment. For those who are inexperienced or less skilled in online teaching, TOM's "show and tell" approach offered favourable conditions for situated and authentic context for learning (Gurley 2018). The open and non-judgmental characteristics of the meetups encouraged the latter group to step out of their comfort zone and become more proactive in taking up new teaching practices demonstrated by their colleagues.

Sessions Stay Relevant to the Changing Needs

As discussed previously, the online meetups started as a response to educators' need to adopt online teaching best practices, tools and technologies. In particular, technical assistance with online tools was a requisite in the early months of transition where educators needed to grasp the basic functionalities to fulfil their critical teaching duties. For this reason, early sessions mainly focused on inducting participants into using Zoom such as recording classes, changing virtual backgrounds, using whiteboard and breakout rooms, etc. When most participants became confident with Zoom, the meetups started to shift to online collaborative tools such as Google Slides, Jamboard, Mural, and Miro, as those tools were picked up by many educators to facilitate real-time student collaboration. Meanwhile, early adopters explored alternative online conferencing platforms such as Microsoft Teams and Google Hangouts and shared their findings in the meetups. Other topics such as LMS content design and video production were interspersed throughout whenever a common interest was identified. A summary of topics featured in TOM from March to December 2020 can be found in the table below.

Thanks to the relaxing of government restrictions, at the start of 2021, Monash campus restarted and teaching resumed in the classroom. However, due to a large number of international students stranded offshore, a new hybrid teaching model was required in order to accommodate both in-class and online students.

Table 1. TOM session topics (March-December, 2020)

2020 sessions	A summary of topics
March	• Zoom on recording video, breakout room, whiteboard and apply virtual background • Google slides/doc as collaborative tool • Whimsical for mind mapping • Share Micro credential site • Introducing Google Hangout for students to chat out of the online class
April	• Zoom issue (recording), breakout room, annotate function useful for collaborative activity • Using H5P in Moodle for interactive activity • Teaching reflection using Zoom, Discord, Whimsical and Google Slides • Comparison between Google Hangout, Google Meet, Zoom and Jamboard
May	• Reflection on User Experience (UX) • Cultural Heroes online collaborative activities • How to activate Closed Captioned in Zoom • Quick start and testing using Microsoft Teams, testing activity using MS Teams • Collaborative tools, Slack, Miro, new features in Moodle
June	• Test activity using Miro • Ice breaking activity using Zoom breakout room and chat • Process of creating and reflecting on online quizzes in Moodle. • Student's feedback and challenges in conducting synchronous online workshops • Video production, editing, and post-production processes
July	• Bootcamp PACE Moodle online platform design • New features and package of Microsoft 365 (Monash) • Simulation of online class using Microsoft Teams
August	• Using MS Teams whiteboard and gallery new features; how to share words file (.doc) and PowerPoint via MS Teams • Ice breaker activity via Zoom chat • Introduced Jamboard, a whiteboard tool from Google, and participants tested Jamboard.
September	• Interactive Group activity via Zoom and Google Docs • Whimsical for a collaborative discussion
October	• Sharing session from participants from different faculty and disciplines. • Online Quizzes • Storytelling on screen - sharing session • Teaching online- Challenges and Solutions
November	• Introduce Augmented Reality (AR) and Virtual Reality (VR) • Reflection on Challenges and Solutions • Setting up MS Teams for tutorials classes and student communication
December	• Ice breaking activity • Online activity using Miro • End of the year reflections

Hybrid teaching posed a new set of challenges to many educators who now have to deal with students both online and in the classroom. TOM started with the first 2021 session on hybrid teaching where two educators shared valuable lessons on how they have run their hybrid classes. In this situation, TOM continued to support educators by providing timely topics addressing their most urgent needs.

CONCLUSION

Considerable momentum has been built over the past year from an institute-specific response to education transition to a cross-faculty and university-wide capacity building and collaborative community learning event. The focus of TOM sessions has gone from online teaching to a mix of online, hybrid teaching and emerging issues to meet the changing needs of the university's teaching community. Despite the evolution of formats and topics, the tenets upon which TOM is based stay true — peer support, practice sharing, hands-on testing, regular reflections and building an open space for collaboration.

For colleagues who are starting a peer-supported or community-based capacity building event, we are offering a few additional recommendations based on our 12-month journey discussed so far:

- Staying on top of participants' immediate needs is what keeps the event going. To achieve this, it is essential that organisers not only understand the broader context and the organisation's general challenges, but to keep a close watch on the frontline and be invested in the needs of the audience that they are serving.
- As with running any regular events, an initiative of this nature requires considerable commitment of the organisers over an extended period of time to ensure its continuity. Support from the leadership team is essential for the longevity of the initiative.
- To kick start practice-based sharing, identify and partner with a few early adopters/innovators who are willing to contribute. Use them as a source of influence and to model both ideas and the ethos of the

meetups. When people get a sense of how things can be done, they are more likely to follow suit.

- Keep sessions focused and protect time in each session for substantive discussion and reflection. Sessions in which the 'sharing' dominated over actual participation undermined the sense of community and exchange.
- Finally, take care of those who are reserved or hesitant to contribute. It always helps to encourage them to step out of their comfort zone, even just by taking a small step.

REFERENCES

Anto, Arkato Gendole; Fer Coenders. "Facilitator and Peer Support in Collaborative Curriculum Design." In: Pieters J., Voogt J., Pareja Roblin N. (eds) *Collaborative Curriculum Design for Sustainable Innovation and Teacher Learning*. Springer, Cham, (2019). https://doi.org/10.1007/978-3-030-20062-6_12.

Chamberlain, Patricia. "Treatment Foster Care." In *Juvenile Justice Bulletin*. Juvenile Justice Clearinghouse, 1998.

Ferguson, Rebecca; Simon Buckingham Shum. "Social Learning Analytics: Five Approaches." *Educational Technology & Society*, 15, no. 3, (2012), 3–26. https://doi:10.1145/2330601.2330616.

Gasevic, Dragan. "COVID-19: The Steep Learning Curve for Online Education." *Monash University Lens*. Last modified April 26, (2020). https://lens.monash.edu/@education/2020/04/26/1380195/COVID-19-the-steep-learning-curve-for-online-education.

Geoghegan, Will. "Stuck at The Barricades: Can Information Really Enter The Mainstream of Teaching and Learning?" *Change.*, 27, no. 2, (1995), 22-30.

Goodyear, Peter, Gilly Salmon, Jonathan Michael Spector, Christine Steeples, Sue Tickner. "Competencies For Online Teaching: A Special Report." *Educational Technology Research and Development.*, 49, no. 1, (2001), 65-72. https://doi:10.1007/BF02504508.

Gurley, Lisa E. "Educators' Preparation to Teach, Perceived Teaching Presence, and Perceived Teaching Presence Behaviors in Blended and Online Learning Environments." *Online Learning.*, 22, no. 2, (2018), 197-220. https://doi:10.24059/olj.v22i2.1255.

Hurst, Beth, Randall Wallace, Sarah B. Nixon. "The Impact of Social Interaction on Student Learning." *Reading Horizons: A Journal of Literacy and Language Arts*, 52, no. 4, (2013), 375-398. https://scholarworks.wmich.edu/reading_horizons/vol52/iss4/5.

Lapointe, Loralee, Marcy Reisetter. "Belonging online: Students' Perceptions of the Value and Efficacy of an Online Learning Community." *International journal on e-learning*, 7, no. 4, (2008), 641.

Lock, Jennifer; Carol Johnson. "Learning from Transitioning to New Technology that Supports Online and Blended Learning: A Case Study." In *Proceedings of E-Learn: World Conference on E-Learning*, (2016), 184-192. Washington, DC, United States: Association for the Advancement of Computing in Education (AACE). https://www.learntechlib.org/primary/p/173938/.

Mallinson, Brenda Justine, Greig Krull. "Building Academic Staff Capacity to Support Online Learning in Developing Countries." *Journal of Asynchronous Learning Network*, 17, no. 2, (2015), 63-72. https://10.24059/olj.v17i2.343.

Mead, Shery; Chery MacNeil. "Peer Support: What Makes it Unique?" *International Peer Support*. December, 2004. http://citeseerx.ist.psu.edu/viewdoc/download?doi=10.1.1.584.6618&rep=rep1&type=pdf.

Mpofu, Nhlanhla. "Online and In the Classroom, COVID-19 has Put New Demands on Teachers." *The Conversation*. Last modified October 4, 2020. https://theconversation.com/online-and-in-the-classroom-COVID-19-has-put-new-demands-on-teachers-147202.

Mucharraz y Cano, Y., Francesco Venuti. "Online Learning Can Still Be Social: 10 Keys to Building a Supportive Digital Community of Learners." *Harvard Business Publishing Education*. Last modified March 25, 2020. https://hbsp.harvard.edu/inspiring-minds/online-learning-can-still-be-social.

Murphy, Mary C., Kathryn Boucher, Christine Logel. "How to Help Students Feel a Sense of Belonging During the Pandemic." *The Greater Good*. Last modified January 19, 2021. https://greatergood.berkeley. edu/article/item/how_to_help_students_feel_a_sense_of_belonging_du ring_the_pandemic.

Paulin, Drew, Caroline Haythornthwaite. "Crowdsourcing the Curriculum: Redefining E-Learning Practices Through Peer-Generated Approaches." *School of Information Studies - Faculty Scholarship*, 173, (2016). https://surface.syr.edu/istpub/173.

Peacock, Susi, John Cowan. "Promoting Sense of Belonging in Online Learning Communities of Inquiry in Accredited Courses: Importance to Learners of Having Sense of Belonging. *Journal of asynchronous learning networks JALN*, 23, no. 2, (2019), 67.

Peersman, Greet, Gillian Fletcher. "Peer Support Approaches: To What Extent are They Appropriate, Acceptable, Beneficial? What is Needed To Implement Them Well? A Systematic Review of Systematic Reviews of International Literature" *The Australia and New Zealand School of Government (ANZSOG)*, with research input from Alice Macfarlan, Sara Rahman, and Keryn Hassall. Melbourne. 2019. https://www.arts.unsw.edu.au/sites/default/files/documents/Peer%20su pport%20approaches.pdf.

Penney, Darby. *Defining "Peer Support": Implications for Policy, Practice, and Research*. Advocates for Human Potential, Inc. (AHPNET). 2018. https://www.ahpnet.com/AHPNet/media/AHPNetMediaLibrary/ White%20Papers/DPenney_Defining_peer_support_2018_Final.pdf.

Penney, Derby, Mead, S., Laura Prescott. *Starting Peer Support: A Manual For People with Mental Health and Physical Health Issues. Draft Technical Assistance Manual*. Rockville, MD: Substance Abuse and Mental Health Services Administration, U.S. Department of Health and Human Services, 2008.

Riessman, Frank. *Restructuring Help: A Human Services Paradigm for the 1990's*. New York: National Self-help Clearinghouse, 1990. https://doi.org/10.1007/BF00931302.

Rogers, E. M. *Diffusion of Innovations.* 5th ed. New York: The Free Press, 2003.

Thomas, Lisa, James Herbert, Marko Teras. "A sense of Belonging to Enhance Participation, Success and Retention in Online programs." *The International Journal of the First Year in Higher Education,* 5, no. 2, (2014), 69-80. https://doi:10.5204/intjfyhe.v5i2.233.

Topping, K. J. "The Effectiveness of Peer Tutoring in Further and Higher Education: A Typology and Review of the Literature." *High Education,* 32, (1996), 321–345. https://doi.org/10.1007/BF00138870.

Wilson, Gail, Elizabeth Stacey. "Online Interaction Impacts on Learning: Teaching the Teachers to Teach Online." *Australasian Journal of Educational Technology,* 20, no. 1, (2004), https://doi.org/10. 14742/ajet.1366.

Wrobleski, Tanya, Gill Walker, Avital Jarus-Hakak, Melinda. J. Suto. "Peer Support as a Catalyst for Recovery: A Mixed-methods Study." *Canadian Journal of Occupational Therapy,* 82, no. 1, (2015), 64-73. https://doi: 10.1177/0008417414551784.

In: The Impact of COVID-19 on Teaching …   ISBN: 978-1-53619-947-5
Editors: S. Studente, S. Ellis et al.   © 2021 Nova Science Publishers, Inc.

Chapter 2

TOWARDS A DIGITAL PEDAGOGY OF INCLUSIVE ACTIVE DISTANCE LEARNING

Helen Caldwell[1,], DProf, Emma Whewell[1], PhD,
Cristina Devecchi[1], PhD, Mary Quirke[2]
and Conor McGukin[2], PhD*

[1]University of Northampton, Northampton, United Kingdom
[2]Trinity College Dublin, Dublin, Ireland, United Kingdom

ABSTRACT

This chapter focuses upon the concept of Active Distance Learning [ADL] as a pedagogical approach to designing and teaching in a remote learning setting. This concept has been developed at the University of Northampton to complement their pedagogical approach of Active Blended Learning. ADL combines sense-making activities with focused and engaging interactions in synchronous and asynchronous online settings. It engages students in knowledge construction, reflection and critique, the development of learner autonomy and the achievement of learning outcomes. The chapter also draws upon the Universal Design for Learning Framework for making ADL inclusive. This approach enables learning to be designed or modified for the greatest diversity of learners

_____

[*] Corresponding Author's E-mail: helen.caldwell@northampton.ac.uk.

possible. This chapter is aligned with contemporary social constructivist, constructionist and connectivist learning theories that emphasise the social situatedness of learning in communities of practice where learners feel empowered to co-create knowledge. Key pedagogical approaches are mapped with the affordances of a range of digital tools to exemplify inclusive ADL practice. A set of vignettes from practice demonstrates digital pedagogies and tools in action, showing how they can add pace, collaboration and engagement to synchronous and asynchronous online learning.

INTRODUCTION

This chapter presents a selection of vignettes from practice to consider how they represent key pedagogic aspects of Active Distance Learning [ADL] through their uses of digital technologies. ADL is an approach to the design of online learning that has been explored across a number of online education courses at the University of Northampton, including the online MA Education, and was extended across other courses when on campus teaching was suspended due to COVID19. The development of ADL in our education courses followed the implementation of a pedagogical model of Active Blended Learning [ABL] that has been in place across the institution since 2014. An aim of ABL is to enhance student engagement through active learning strategies alongside a move to a new campus without lecture theatres (Palmer, Lomer and Bashliyska, 2017; Armellini, Antunes and Howe, 2021; Rodriguez and Armellini, 2021). It is characterised by a digitally rich learning environment and collaboration between students in knowledge construction through interaction with content, peers and tutors (University of Northampton 2020). In designing online courses for teachers and students and in revising existing ABL content to make it fully online, we have aimed to keep these principles in mind, and we have used the term ADL to describe our teaching and learning strategies. This chapter also explores the relationship between Universal Design for Learning [UDL] and ADL, and how this can create more inclusive online learning environments.

THEORETICAL BACKGROUND

The notion of active learning has its roots in constructivism that emphasises learners' active engagement with knowledge building (Cummings, Mason, Shelton and Baur, 2017). Papert's constructionist theories add an extra layer by suggesting that digital environments can enable learners to develop ideas by constructing meaningful digital artefacts (Papert, 1980; Harel and Papert, 1991). Although these ideas date back to the development of Logo in the 1960s they anticipate the emergence of today's maker movement. Interestingly, the term Logo derives from the Greek word *logos* meaning 'thought' and Papert coined the phrase 'objects to think with' to describe a creative process that bridges physical and abstract spheres.

We can also draw theoretical underpinnings from the links between social interaction and learning (Vygotsky, 1978), together with the idea of communities of practice engaging in joint enterprise around shared goals (Wenger, 1998), and the concept of communities of inquiry linking cognitive, social and teaching presence (Garrison, Anderson and Archer, 2000). As Young and Tseng (2008) point out, studying an online community requires an understanding of the physical as well as the virtual contexts, and this may be especially true for communities of teachers. Online learning communities allow a merge of real and virtual worlds as participants engage in discussions about real practice in the virtual world. The online community represents a continual crossover between these two spheres, and this may be mediated by the shared artefacts (Burnett, 2016). Social online learning often involves a process of participation and reification; in other words, 'making something real,' identified by Wenger (1998). Goggins et al., (2011) describe this process:

> 'Participation involves acting and interacting, and reification involves producing artefacts (such as tools, words, symbols, rules, documents, concepts, theories, and so on) around which the negotiation of meaning is organized.' (Goggins et al., 2011 p. 210).

An area in need of further consideration, they suggest, is how the technology tools mediate social and intellectual engagement within a community (Goggins et al., 2011 p. 224). This invites us to consider the role of posted comments, media, and digital artefacts in articulating pedagogy and practice, and the possibility that they might act as anchors for the further evolution of ideas within the community (Caldwell, Whewell and Heaton, 2020).

The idea of networked communication has become part of everyday life and is increasingly integrated into collaborative learning environments as a form of social constructionism, recognising that the social context creates a richer environment for learning (Stevens, Boden and Rekowski, 2013; May and Mumby 2004; Kafai and Burke, 2013). Like constructionism, connectivist models recognise the role of digital technologies in learning. They suggest that the virtual and physical worlds are interconnected rather than independent (Young and Tseng, 2008), describing the shifting nature of knowledge as patterns of connections are formed and reformed, and as ideas are co-constructed through social interactions (Siemens, 2005). Connectivism emphasises the links between people and digital resources (Siemens, 2005; Downes, 2010), taking account of the fact that tacit knowledge can be encoded in digital artefacts (Nilmanat, 2011) and that information shared by participants may be drawn from either:

> 'Connectivist models explicitly rely on the ubiquity of networked connections between people, digital artifacts, and content' (Anderson and Dron, 2011, p. 87).

Research in the field also notes ways in which that active learning implies that learners will take responsibility for their own learning (Godlewska et al., 2019; Armellini et al., 2021). Moreover, it is recognised that active learning methodologies that involve authentic tasks lead to deeper engagement and deeper cognitive processing (Jeong et al., 2019). Traxler suggests that in an online environment it is important to remain flexible, to seek connections, and to retain learner agency and authenticity (Traxler, 2018).

The idea of 'learning by doing' in a digital environment, and then making this process explicit by thinking and talking is central to ADL as learners engage in making sense of ideas by explicitly representing them and building upon them through dialogue. Knowledge construction takes place through technology-enabled exchanges and social interactions mediated by technology tools and tangible outputs. In many of our examples learners engage with content in active dynamic ways that result in shareable products that evoke responses.

Also key to ADL is the interplay between personalised learning and collective knowledge construction. ADL aims to be student centered and to value student voice, whilst seeking to create discursive environments where learners feel empowered to co-create knowledge. The knowledge building process can be described as rhizomatic in that it is evolutionary and fluid in response to the learning community (Cormier, 2014; Deleuze and Guattari, 1988; Bozkurt, et al., 2016). An aim is to mobilise dispersed groups to learn with and from each other in nurtured communities. However, this aim is not without its challenges, and online learners may become increasingly disconnected, tending towards lurking, losing presence and eventually dropping out (Mackness and Bell, 2015).

In summary, the ADL examples that follow are aligned with contemporary social constructivist, constructionist and connectivist learning theories that emphasise the social situatedness of learning. They illustrate that it is important to share what knowledge and knowing looks and feels like in an online space, and through this to build epistemic cognition amongst learners (Cope and Kolantzis, 2009). They demonstrate that establishing strong online communities increases the engagement and enjoyment of learning at a distance. The making of digital artefacts can add pace to learning and prompt re-discussion and re-mixing of content, resulting in an evolutionary, non-linear learning process. A typical learning journey within such social online communities moves in and out of cognitive, digital and physical domains as participants articulate ideas through various modes of representation. In a creative and social online learning environment, rich collective content and shared understandings can represent connections between thoughts, spaces, time and content (Caldwell, Whewell and Heaton, 2020).

UNIVERSAL DESIGN FOR LEARNING (UDL)

This section examines Universal Design for Learning (UDL) and the potential of its relationship with ADL as we seek to be inclusive in designing online learning. The world of education has radically changed over the past year, and consequently a model of 'universal and active inclusion' is being embraced as the new norm. A key part of this emerging agenda is the application of UDL philosophies and practices to online educational opportunities.

UDL has its origins in the principles of Universal Design (UD); an approach that emanated from the architectural and built environment disciplines and is defined by seven key principles that seek to guide all designs '... to be usable to the greatest extent possible by people of all ages and abilities.' (Story, Mueller, and Mace, 1998, p. 2). Key UD thinking, and actions have been successfully adapted to the world of learning through several frameworks, with some necessary and bespoke modifications and additions to the original seven principles.

Whilst several different UDL frameworks have emerged, the CAST framework is perhaps the most well-known and applied (https://udlguidelines.cast.org). The CAST guidelines were originally influenced by UD, Vygotskian thought, and neuroscience research. They seek to offer a framework for the implementation of UDL around three paradigms:

- the 'what' (multiple means of representation),
- the 'why' (multiple means of engagement), and
- the 'how' (multiple means of action and expression) of learning (CAST, 2018).

UDL promotes successful and active learning processes by advocating for the considered design of learning environments, for the diversity of learners that engage in our educational programmes (Rose and Meyer, 2006). This goes way beyond the traditional considerations that many appreciate for those learners with a disability, in that it seeks to appreciate all conceivable individual differences in our student population (e.g., second language learners, non-traditional students). Therefore, active inclusion practices are at the very core of UDL practice. Fundamentally, a UDL approach necessitates that online learning environments are designed from the very outset to be as inclusive as possible, minimising but never negating the need for add-on support entirely, as a learner may require reasonable adjustments in a grouped or individualised manner.

Both UD and UDL emerged from the 'social model' of disability – a perspective that has successfully argued that inclusion cannot be achieved without acknowledging that changes are required regarding how society organises itself – i.e., that the way in which society is organised disables the person. A simple way to appreciate UDL and its approach is to remember that its central objective is to design for the possibility for every individual to engage in an active manner in a fully inclusive educational environment. This necessitates a similar shift of thinking as when considering the medical and social models of disability (Quirke and Mc Guckin, 2019).

However, the application of UDL thinking should not assume that it is only for those learners who have a disability – doing so would be exclusive and become a contradiction. Thus, this 'thinking' about 'designing for active inclusion' shifts the focus as to how we might "… consider universal design [as] a process, rather than [as] an achievement …" (Story et al., 1998, p. 2). With the very best of intentions, many practitioners often believe they are taking an inclusive approach in their course development and interactions with their learners. However, we should acknowledge that this is generally done in an unintentional and unplanned manner. The trick is, as argued by Quirke and McCarthy (2020), to acknowledge that 'inclusion is everybody's business' and that change should be planned and be intentional from the conception. The difference between adopting an intentional approach [or not] becomes even more critical when we consider the affordances that inclusive learning environments can offer in online modes. Moreover, the consideration of active learning opportunities for the virtual world and the need to intentionally design it to be inclusive in and of itself, while continuing to recognise the need for individual and grouped supports, is a critical part of the 'active' inclusive learning agenda.

It is evident that we need to consider how we define and action 'inclusive practice' in the virtual world and subsequently in the contemporary 'inclusive virtual learning environment' for the diversity of learners that we meet on our courses. As a relatively new concept, Edyburn (2010) reminds us that 'The allure of UDL has captured the imagination of many educators and policy makers.' (p. 33) with literature '… starting to give definition and shape to what a UD educational model-based project or intervention looks like …' (Rao, Ok, and Bryant, 2014. p. 164). Together with ADL, an active and well-considered approach to UDL can give definition and shape as to what a virtual inclusive learning environment can be, how it will operate, and not just for those that require grouped supports but moreover, be exploited, for a greater diversity of learner.

The first vignette from practice in the section below describes how UDL guidelines were applied as a weekly research group at Trinity College Dublin moved online during COVID19.

MAPPING PEDAGOGICAL APPROACHES

This section presents a number of vignettes from practice drawn from higher education provision at the University of Northampton and Trinity College Dublin, and maps them with examples of pedagogical techniques associated with ADL and UDL. The vignettes demonstrate a range of tools that were employed to improve student experience and engagement in online learning. They are related to aspects of learning such as inclusion, sensemaking, student engagement, learner experience, communities of practice and collective knowledge building. Pedagogical techniques associated with ADL evolve from well-known distance learning approaches which often include;

- Online learning tools
- Flipped learning
- MOOCs and online courses
- Learning management systems
- Education and Gaming
- Mixing and matching digital tools. (Traxler, 2018)

ADL builds upon these techniques to embrace learners as part of the process, offering authentic asynchronous and synchronous opportunities for learner generated content creation. Examples of participatory practice include:

- Use of polls, chat, video and microphones
- Collaborative digital tools embedded in resources
- Cooperative and team-based learning using breakout rooms
- Simulations and augmented reality to promote inquiry, debate and case study-based learning
- Collaborative project-based learning.

A colleague explains their adjustment to remote learning in 2020; 'In the early planning stages we talked about the importance of online learning not being just the students accessing a LE via their laptops or mobile phones. It had to be a different style of learning and needed to incorporate collaboration, accountability and a feeling of belonging to a community. This was at the heart of all our online sessions.'

Vignette 1: An Inclusive Learning Experience

As ADL and UDL are merged, it is timely to reflect on 'inclusive practice' and what that means for the virtual world, and in particular how this new model can be fundamental to the very application of inclusive thinking for virtual learning.

Moving a research group that meets weekly online was a challenge when COVID arrived. The Inclusion in Education and Society Research Group in the Trinity College Dublin planned to re-establish itself in a virtual world, while continuing to espouse the values of UDL and inclusion. As each week was prepared in terms of content, the needs of a diverse audience and speakers had to be considered to ensure that all had a successful learning and personal experience. As noted by the convenor of the group (Dr Patricia McCarthy), 'One of the things we were trying to achieve was to ensure a sense of community was maintained during the pandemic – while also exploring theory and practice emerging around inclusion.' Each week a speaker was engaged, briefed, and the ethos discussed. Consideration was given to a variety of issues, including the platform used, content, pacing, timing, structure, and additional features (e.g., chat functionality being used appropriately). A decision was made at an early point to not record – allowing for open conversation. Inclusive practices have been exploited by ways of considered use of imagery (alt text used where possible), terminology and language considerations (to ensure optimum learning and engagement for all), and moreover a subtle demand for researchers engaging to consider 'inclusive practice' not just in terms of their research but also their very engagements. The group has grown, and participants are varied; from academic professors to learners with a disability (including intellectual disability); colleagues from other disciplines, other colleges, and even other countries. Maintaining an active and inclusive ethos is a continuous and very conscious effort - but this will ensure equality of outcome and a more sustainable research agenda in line with UN SDG goals (e.g., SDG4: Quality Education, SDG10: Reduced Inequalities).

Vignette 2: Sensemaking through Remaking and Reconceptualising Digital Artefacts

Sensemaking is integral to ADL as students interpret ideas and demonstrate their understanding. It involves an interplay of 'action and interpretation,' thinking about organising and categorising learning, and allowing for agency and flow (Weick, Sutcliff and Obstfeld, 2005, p. 409). It takes small steps forwards as ideas are reconceptualised and re-represented. The example below demonstrates how higher education students might remodel, reinterpret and re-order existing material. Independence is central to sensemaking and this activity allowed students to experiment with their digital artefacts, design them as they see fit and in a way in which they felt would best communicate the material. These serve as catalysts for further reflections and reinterpretations within the online community.

With students who would be using Padlet as a tool for evaluating learning my aim was to ensure that they understood the full potential of all the tools that Padlet has to offer. With this in mind, I made a Padlet with a post for each individual tool available within Padlet, fifteen in all. Students were asked to remake this Padlet, claiming it as their own, and then systematically use each tool, editing each post to add an example. This moved them from the familiar: adding a post, an image, a link; to the unfamiliar: adding an audio comment, a screen recording, a screenshot, a map, using the searches available within and outside Padlet and changing the appearances of posts, text in posts and the background and cover image. I also made a Padlet in the canvas format with some summary posts of different theories and approaches to using digital technology in learning and some examples from practice (Figure 1). Suggested reading supported students to investigate learning theory further. This activity gave them a clear scaffold but also pushed them to investigate everything they could do with Padlet, something that would be vital when they came to use it in their assignments.

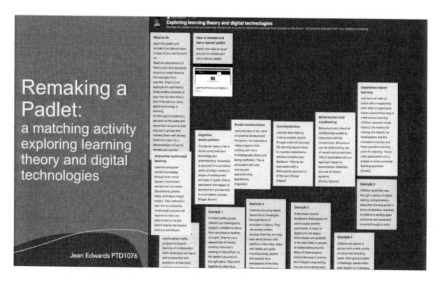

Figure 1. Remaking a Padlet.

Vignette 3: Working in Small Groups to Co-Construct Knowledge within an Online Community of Practice

A distinctive feature of ADL is its active nature. To achieve this, good ADL practices make use of a variety of digital tools to re-create online the experience and benefits of belonging to a community of practice (Lave and Wenger 1991). An online community allows learners to construct, build and share knowledge across time zones and countries and offers control over their pace, type and location of engagement (Caldwell, Whewell and Heaton, 2020). Lecturers can draw upon the community's rhizomatic potential to enable multiple groups of learners to tackle tasks. In this way, being active means to foster learners' engagement and interaction through teamwork and collaboration as they learn together in a shared domain. Vignette 3 demonstrates a sustained commitment to building a sense of a community of learners. By assigning tasks that can be completed asynchronously, learners are encouraged to reflect and respond critically. Within these virtual communities, learners are engaged in multiple and varied learning spaces which re-create online the affective and emotional experience of being together physically. The individual and collaborative activities overlap and might be described as convergent ecologies of learning (Sangrà, et al., 2019). The combined physical, social and cognitive spaces develop both social and independent learning skills, via a flexible, anywhere and anytime learning experience.

This maths masterclass was held on Zoom meetings with around 70 participants. They were able to display their cameras and post comments. Having their cameras visible allowed me to see what they were doing, provide feedback, clarify instructions, and change pace if necessary. I created a team-based activity, referencing aspects of the preceding five disparately-themed sessions in the form of an online treasure hunt: the students were split up into teams, randomly, using Zoom's breakout rooms. Each team was given a URL which took them to an activity created using H5P (an open-source tool for creating interactive HTML5 content).

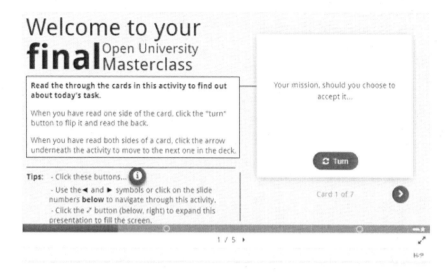

Figure 2. H5P interactive content for an interactive maths workshop.

Achieving an appropriate score on tasks revealed portions of text which could be concatenated to find the URL of the second task (which worked similarly to find the third, and so on). My role during the session involved moving between breakout rooms providing support and occasional hints. Whilst doing so I saw (and congratulated) emergent digital collaboration solutions. Some students worked on spreadsheets or word processing documents while one screen-shared. Others used collaborative environments to work directly on the same document whilst continuing discussions via Zoom.

Vignette 4: Social and Intellectual Engagement within a Community

In Vignette 4 the use of discussion boards alongside synchronous discussions facilitated joint exploration of topics, leading to greater depth of community building. An integral member of the community, the teacher is present to provide support and feedback, add to the discussion and model the learning process but also able to stand back.

When planning my module on the Online MAEd at the University of Northampton, I considered how I would engage students outside of taught sessions and support an active community of practice. I started by considering how I could encourage students to reflect on what was to be taught and decided that having pre-sessional tasks would be beneficial. Pre-sessional tasks are often posted on a discussion board within the online learning platform and consist of tasks such as asking students to watch a short video or engage with reading with carefully planned questions to encourage critical thinking and reflection in relation to students' personal professional experiences. To support the development of an online community, I respond to posts made by students, identifying positive points raised as well as asking questions to deepen critical thinking. Students are encouraged to respond to each other (Figure 3). This virtual communication not only enhances students' understanding of the subject, but also the rapport of the group when engaging with each other during the online taught sessions.

5.2 Pre sessional task 2

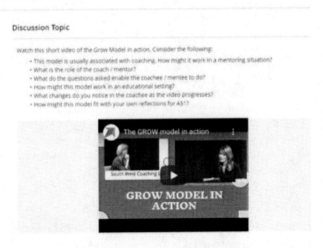

Figure 3. An example of a pre-sessional task to inspire an online discussion.

Each session follows the same structure, from the pre-sessional tasks, to something to think about, which usually starts the online taught session, to materials used during online teaching and finishing with a post-sessional task. This structure supports students' knowledge construction, critical thinking skills and sensemaking through consolidating learning during the post-tasks and asynchronous discussion boards. Being consistent with structure provides familiarity for students as well as expectations of student engagement being clear. The structure helps to make a smooth transition between the synchronous and asynchronous discussions.

Vignette 5: Creating Collaboratively Online

Contextualised experiential learning opportunities and constructing knowledge together are key features of ADL, and offer increased student autonomy and engagement, potential for cross pollination of ideas and a sense of purpose (Caldwell, 2018). Vignette 5 demonstrates the use of a live shared Powerpoint where students are working synchronously on the content of a Powerpoint slide in a breakout room. The teacher can move between the breakout rooms as well as monitoring the groups' progress on the shared document. This scenario illustrates peer to peer online learning, wherein the teacher becomes a facilitator of shared knowledge creation and can support students effectively where needed.

When working with PowerPoint Online the presentation can be shared with a group allowing a collaborative use of the slides. Planning for this, I set up a PowerPoint presentation with a 'model' or 'scaffold' slide at the beginning and a reference list slide at the end. In between these I had enough slides for students working in pairs to have one each. I shared the presentation with the students as viewers as we talked about the learning activity and discussed what they would be doing to prepare and make their slide. I either provided an example slide for them to use as a model, or we devised a scaffold together based on earlier activity in the session. Students were then put in pairs in breakout rooms, so they could work together, one pair allocated to each slide.

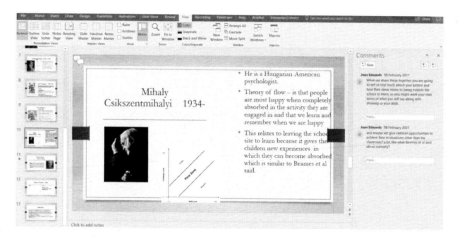

Figure 4. Students collaborating to create a set of slides with tutor support.

I was able to see students working on their slide/s 'live' as they added text and other material, using the slide sorter view to keep an overview of how the learning was progressing and identifying where I might need to focus my support. I could then go to individual slides and use the comment function to prompt, ask questions and give feedback or provide this in conversation within the breakout groups. It was the closest to circulating around the class and working with pairs and groups face-to-face that I have experienced so far. Students found this activity engaging and seemed to enjoy the sense of 'live' interaction it supported. It gave them a sense of momentum and pace.

Vignette 6: Enhancing Student Experience and Skills through Virtual Placements

Collaborative content creation allows learning to evolve out of social behaviours and engagement with others. ADL can involve an interplay of personal and collective knowledge building, and critical thinking is often an outcome of this. Within the virtual community in this example the teacher is both visible and invisible, distant and close. The teacher's role is that of 'sketching' what is to be accomplished whilst giving space and freedom to the learners to add depth and detail to the direction of travel.

A range of 'virtual' placement days were offered as alternatives to face-to-face placements. The following is an example of a single placement day which was developed on Behaviour Management and Executive Functions for second year students. An online, visual collaboration platform called Miro was used to host the session (Figure 5).

Students had to watch a You Tube clip which captures some of children's more humorous behaviour and then cast a vote, via a coloured post it, on whether they regard children to be 'mischievous or inquisitive?' Students then completed a behaviour management skills audit via a link to Google Forms. This provided students with questions which would help them reflect on their own experiences of behaviour management and highlight any areas for development. Once the Behaviour Management Skills Audit was completed it was sent directly to the students. This then enabled students to refer to this form for the next task.

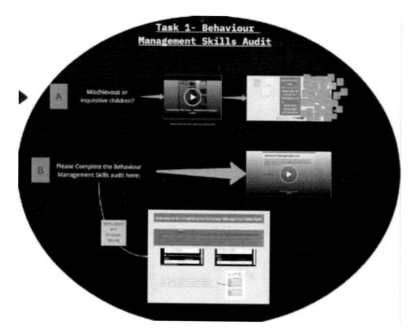

Figure 5. Using a MIRO board to develop a virtual placement.

The final question of the Behaviour Management Skills Audit asked students to select five areas that they would like to learn more about in relation to behaviour management. Referring to their e-mailed version of the Behaviour Management Skills Audit, students were then asked to follow the hyper-links to more information regarding their chosen areas and make notes to inform their practice in future. The final activity involved a mini course which would help students begin to understand why Executive Functions are important in relation to children's behaviour. The task involved four parts, where students were asked to navigate a readable Word document within the Miro Board, before contributing a comment or resource.

Vignette 7: A Student's Perspective of Student Engagement and Learner Experience

Engaging in online learning can be challenging. During COVID-19 as educators we were faced with trying to understand the factors which impact upon student engagement and disengagement and their sense of embodiment within the remote environment.

We were aware that it may have been an isolating and difficult time for many learners, and being expected to be part of a community of learners and to show autonomy in their learning choices may have been challenging. This vignette is written from a student perspective. It acknowledges some challenges but also suggests that ADL offers choices and greater freedom within a digital environment, meaningful interaction with other learners, collaborative opportunities, increased authenticity, and potential for thoughtful responses to course content (Caldwell, Whewell and Heaton, 2020).

In studying an online MA Education course, I have experienced several digital pedagogies which have been used to enhance our ADL. Interaction between students and lecturers, and among students themselves, is perhaps less natural with remote learning, particularly when cameras and microphones are frequently unused. Alternative approaches are required to encourage interaction, one of the most common of which is the use of breakout rooms. Breakout rooms provided me with a more intimate and less intimidating environment for discussion. Other tools can be used to not only encourage interaction and engagement but support learner autonomy. My sessions have featured several tools such as Jamboard, Padlet and Mentimeter. These tools enable collective knowledge building and real-time remote collaboration. Students can post ideas of work onto these forums and simultaneously view and comment on other students' posts. I have found these tools to be very effective in increasing my engagement with the learning. Tools such as Google Classroom and Google Slides have also enabled my tutors to create digital environments in the absence of physical environments. For example, when teaching about health and safety in physical education, a virtual sports hall featuring Bitmoji characters provided a visual demonstration of common hazards (Figure 6).

ADL offers me a range of ways that I can engage with the learning. I can choose the environment in which I learn, whether this be at home, in an educational setting or elsewhere. In many respects I have found ADL to be more accessible as it allows more flexibility for how and where to learn.

Figure 6. Bitmoji Sports hall hazard-building activity.

Vignette 8: Building Graduate Skills through a Simulated Physical Placement Setting

Inclusive ADL can create the space for learners to develop and refine a range of hard and soft skills leading to the establishment of long lasting, much sought-after graduate competencies. Regarding the social dimension, good ADL practice supports teamwork and collaboration. This vignette draws upon virtual reality to create a simulated placement. By requiring individuals to work in teams, it fosters learners' time management, cooperation, sense of responsibility and appreciation of the importance of interdependence within a virtual, but nonetheless real community of learning. ADL offers potential for widening access to higher education, developing employability skills and lifelong learning.

As a result of the COVID-19 pandemic students have been unable to attend a physical placement setting. To support both knowledge and practice, a virtual placement experience was created. Students completed daily tasks to support them in understanding their wider role within a setting, for example, exploring the role of professionals and what contributes to an enabling environment through the exploration of an interactive virtual learning platform. For each daily task the students were expected to upload their progress to enable them to contribute to discussion boards as well as enable them to reflect on how they had met aspects of the Graduate Practitioner Competencies. Due to the flexibility of the placement, students could complete their tasks at their own pace whilst supporting each other such as the use of peer assessment to reflect on each other's lesson plans in relation to inclusion and diversity, choosing the appropriate medium to share their planned session with wider professionals.

Figure 7. Inside a virtual reality classroom.

Although the project has been challenging such as not being able to physically experience a physical setting, it has been rewarding for students and the Early Years team. Students were able to explore the Early Years Virtual Learning Environment which supported them to consider a real setting in practice. This was of particular benefit to the first year Early Childhood students where the majority had never experienced an education setting. Whilst exploring the environment, the students were able to consider the application of policies such as health and safety and consider risk management strategies. Feedback has included: 'Being able to work the activities in when it best suited me due to my work hours extending and still gaining from the experience…even though I work in a setting already it furthered my knowledge that I then could take back to work and also informed my colleagues.'

The virtual placement enabled the students to gain knowledge which was difficult to gain due to the pandemic and this demonstrates that although a 'real setting is beneficial' to aid experience, an online community can still support and develop students holistically to aid their transferability into their future pathway.

CONCLUSION

This chapter has discussed ADL and UDL as pedagogical approaches to online learning in relation to a selection of vignettes from recent HE practice. As the vignettes exemplify, ADL combines sense-making activities with focused and engaging interactions in synchronous and asynchronous online settings. It focuses on engaging students in knowledge construction, reflection and critique, the development of learner autonomy and the achievement of learning outcomes through communities of practice.

We demonstrate how the UDL framework can be used alongside ADL to enhance online inclusivity. This approach enables learning to be designed or modified for the greatest diversity of learners possible. It is based on the idea of offering multiple opportunities for engagement, representation, and action and expression in online learning environments, and providing choice in how learners access information and display their learning. Moore et al., (2018), suggest that multimodal learning allows learners to 'represent, record and reflect on their own learning through visuals, dialogues and written texts' (Moore et al., 2018, p. 45). Choice about how to and when to engage with learning offers inclusivity and autonomy which can support learners with a wide range of needs and preferences.

Inclusive ADL offers learners and educators many distinct advantages when working online. Despite inevitable technological challenges it is not bound by some of the physical, time and geographical restrictions that face-to-face learning presents. Digital tools effectively facilitate sharing, and the cyclical making and talking, posting and responding that takes place synchronously and asynchronously within online communities can positively enhance learning. Digital posts and artefacts can act as stepping-stones for re-discussion, re-making and re-mixing content. This leads us to summarise the online community knowledge building process as an interplay of three dualities: physical and digital, talking and making, and personal and collective, that describe the interaction between communities, tools, content and pedagogies (Caldwell, Whewell and Heaton, 2020) (See Figure 8). We suggest that there are significant opportunities to develop ADL learning environments that all students can thrive in.

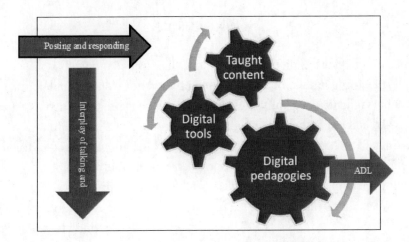

Figure 8. The process of collective knowledge building within an ADL online learning community (adapted from Caldwell, Whewell and Heaton, 2020).

We make the following recommendations when planning learning in an online environment:

- Recognise the process of active and creative social online learning leading to collective knowledge-building
- Use technology tools that allow for multimodal responses that foster inclusivity and allow for responding and remixing to amplify learning within a community
- Embrace a model of universal and active inclusion by creating online learning environments that intentionally address the full diversity of our student populations.

ACKNOWLEDGMENTS

We would like to thank our colleagues who shared their practice and reflections on ADL and UDL by contributing vignettes from practice.

Joanne Barrow: Senior Lecturer, University of Northampton.

Thomas Briggs: Maths and Museums Educator and MA Education Student, University of Northampton.

Jean Edwards: Senior Lecturer, University of Northampton.

Beth Garrett: MA Education Student, University of Northampton.

David Meechan: Senior Lecturer, University of Northampton.

Devon Rossetti: Senior Lecturer, University of Northampton.

Mary Quirke: PhD Researcher, School of Education, Trinity College Dublin.

REFERENCES

Anderson, T. and Dron, J. 2011. Three generations of distance education pedagogy. *The International Review of Research in Open and Distance Learning,* 12(3), pp. 81-97. doi: 10.19173/irrodl.v12i3.890.

Armellini, A., Antunes, V. T. and Howe, R. 2021. Student perspectives on learning experiences in a higher education active blended learning context. *TechTrends,* pp. 1-11. https://link.springer.com/article/10.1007/s11528-021-00593-w.

Bozkurt, A., Honeychurch, S., Caines, A., Bali, M., Koutropoulos, A. and Cormier, D. (2016). Community Tracking in a cMOOC and Nomadic Learner Behavior Identification on a Connectivist Rhizomatic Learning Network. *Turkish Online Journal of Distance Education,* 17(4), pp. 4-30. doi:10.17718/tojde.09231.

Burnett, C. 2016. *The digital age and its implications for learning and teaching in the primary school.* York: Cambridge Primary Review Trust. https://cprtrust.org.uk/wp-content/uploads/2016/07/Burnett-report-20160720.pdf.

Caldwell, H. (2018). Mobile technologies as a catalyst for pedagogic innovation within teacher education. *International Journal of Mobile and Blended Learning, 10*(2), 50–65. doi: 10.4018/IJMBL.2018040105.

Caldwell, H., Whewell, E., and Heaton, R. (2020) The impact of visual posts on creative thinking and knowledge building in an online community of educators. *Thinking skills and Creativity.* 36. doi: 10.1016/j.tsc.2020.100647.

Cope, B. and Kalantzis, M. 2009. Ubiquitous learning: An agenda for educational transformation. In: *Proceedings of the 6th International Conference on Networked Learning*. Lancaster University. pp. 576-582. Available at: http://www.networkedlearningconference.org.uk/past/ nlc2008/abstracts/PDFs/Cope_576-582.pdf (Accessed 30 December 2018).

CAST. 2018. *Universal Design for Learning Guidelines version 2.2*. Retrieved from http://udlguidelines.cast.org.

Cormier, D. 2014. Rhizo14—The MOOC that community built. *The International Journal for Innovation and Quality in Learning*, 2(3). Retrieved from http://papers.efquel.org/index.php/innoqual/article/ view/162/48.

Cummings, C., Mason, D., Shelton, K. and Baur, K. 2017. Active learning strategies for online and blended learning environments. In *Flipped instruction: Breakthroughs in research and practice* (pp. 88-114). IGI Global. doi: 10.4018/978-1-5225-1803-7.ch006.

Deleuze, G. and Guattari, F. 1988. *A thousand plateaus: Capitalism and schizophrenia*. Bloomsbury Publishing.

Downes, S. 2010. New Technology Supporting Informal Learning. *Journal of Emerging Technologies in Web Intelligence*, 2(1). doi: 10.4304/ jetwi.2.1.27-33.

Edyburn, D. L. 2010. Would you recognize universal design for learning if you saw it? Ten propositions for new directions for the second decade of UDL. *Learning Disability Quarterly*, 33(1), 33-41. doi:10.2307/ 25701429.

Garrison, D. R., Anderson, T. and Archer, W. 2000. Critical inquiry in a text-based environment: Computer conferencing in higher education. *The Internet and Higher Education*, 2, 1–19. doi:10.1016/S1096-7516(00)00016-6.

Godlewska, A., Beyer, W., Whetstone, S., Schaefli, L., Rose, J., Talan, B., Kamin-Patterson, S., Lamb, C. and Forcione, M. 2019. Converting a large lecture class to an active blended learning class: Why, how, and what we learned. *Journal of Geography in Higher Education*, 43(1), pp. 96-115. doi: 10.1080/03098265.2019.1570090.

Goggins, S. P., Laffey, J. and Gallagher, M. 2011. Completely online group formation and development: small groups as socio-technical systems. *Information Technology & People*, 24(2), pp. 104-133. DOI: 10.1108/09593841111137322.

Harel, I. E., and Papert, S. E. 1991. *Constructionism*. Stamford, CT: Ablex.

Heaton, R. 2018. *Autoethnography to artography: An exhibition of cognition in artist teacher practice*, PhD diss. University of Cambridge. doi: 10.17863/CAM.33324.

Jeong, J. S., González-Gómez, D., Cañada-Cañada, F., Gallego-Picó, A. and Bravo, J. C. 2019. Effects of active learning methodologies on the students' emotions, self-efficacy beliefs and learning outcomes in a science distance learning course. *Journal of Technology and Science Education*, 9(2), 217-227. doi: 10.3926/jotse.530.

Kafai, Y. B. and Burke, Q. 2013. March. The social turn in K-12 programming: moving from computational thinking to computational participation. In: *Proceeding of the 44th ACM technical symposium on computer science education*, ACM, pp. 603-608.

Lave, J., and Wenger, E. 1991. *Situated learning: Legitimate peripheral participation*. Cambridge, New York: Cambridge University Press.

Mackness, J. and Bell, F. 2015. Rhizo14: A rhizomatic learning cMOOC in sunlight and in shade. *Open Praxis*, 7(1), pp. 25-38. doi:10.5944/openpraxis.7.1.173.

May, S., and Mumby, D. K. (2004). *Engaging Organizational Communication Theory and Research: Multiple Perspectives*. SAGE.

Moore, D., Hoskyn, M. and Mayo, J. 2018. Thinking Language Awareness at a Science Centre: Ipads, science and early literacy development with multilingual, kindergarten children in Canada. *International Journal of Bias, Identity and Diversities in Education* (IJBIDE), 3(1), 40-62. DOI: 10.4018/IJBIDE.2018010104.

Nilmanat, R. 2011. Investigating image usage and tacit knowledge sharing in online communities. *International Journal of Innovation and Learning*, 10(4), pp. 350–364. doi: 10.1504/IJBIS.2015.069430.

Palmer, E., Lomer, S. and Bashliyska, I. 2017. *Overcoming barriers to student engagement in Active Blended Learning*. http://nectar.

northampton.ac.uk/13030/1/Palmer_etal_2017_Overcoming_barriers_t
o_student_engagement_in_Active_Blended_Learning.pdf.

Papert, S. 1980. *Mindstorms: Children, computers, and powerful ideas.* New
York: Basic Books.

Quirke. M, and McCarthy, P. 2020. *A Conceptual Framework of Universal
Design for Learning (UDL) for the Irish Further Education and
Training Sector Where Inclusion is Everybody's Business.*
Dublin: SOLAS. https://www.solas.ie/f/70398/x/948bcabcc4/udl-for-
fet-framework. pdf.

Quirke, M., and Mc Guckin, C. 2019. Career guidance needs to learn from
'disability' if it is to embrace an uncertain future. European Conference
on Educational Research (ECER): *Education in an Era of Risk - The
Role of Educational Research for the Future,* Universität Hamburg,
Hamburg, Germany, 3rd - 6th September, 2019. Abstracts not published.

Rodriguez, B. and Armellini, A. 2021. *Cases on Active Blended Learning in
Higher Education* IGI Global. http://openaccess.uoc.edu/webapps/
o2/bitstream/10609/129986/1/guardia%20et%20al%20chap%2013_pa
dilla%20book.pdf.

Rao, K., Ok, M. W., and Bryant, B. R. 2014. A review of research on
universal design educational models. *Remedial and special education,*
35(3), 153-166. doi: 10.1177/0741932513518980.

Rose, D. H., and Meyer, A. 2006. *A practical reader in universal design for
learning.* Harvard Education Press.

Sangrá, A., Raffaghelli, J. E. and Guitert - Catasús, M. 2019. Learning
ecologies through a lens: Ontological, methodological and applicative
issues. A systematic review of the literature. *British Journal of
Educational Technology, 50*(4), pp. 1619-1638. doi: 10.1111/bjet.
12795.

Siegenthaler, F. 2013. Towards an ethnographic turn in contemporary art
scholarship. *Critical Arts: South-North Cultural and Media Studies,*
27(6), 737-752. doi: 10.1080/02560046.2013.867594.

Siemens, G. 2005. Connectivism: A Learning Theory for the Digital Age.
International Journal of Instructional Technology and Distance

Learning, 2(1), 3–10. https://jotamac.typepad.com/jotamacs_weblog/files/Connectivism.pdf.

Stevens, G., Boden, A. and Von Rekowski, T. 2013. Objects-to-think-with-together. Rethinking Papert's Ideas of Construction Kits for Kids in the Age of Online Sociability. *End-User Development*, pp. 1-7. https://link.springer.com/book/10.1007%2F978-3-642-38706-7.

Story, M. F., Mueller, J. L., and Mace, R. L. 1998. *The universal design file: Designing for people of all ages and abilities.* Raleigh, NC: Center for Universal Design. Retrieved from http://www.ncsu. edu/ncsu/design /cud/pubs_p/pudfiletoc.htm.

Traxler, J. 2018. Distance learning—Predictions and possibilities. *Education Sciences*, 8(1), p. 35. doi: 10.3390/educsci8010035.

University of Northampton. 2020. *Defining Active Blended Learning.* (online) http://www.northampton.ac.uk/ilt/current-projects/defining-abl/.

Vygotsky, L. S. 1978. *Mind in society, the development of higher psychological processes.* Cambridge, MA: Harvard University Press.

Weick, K. E., Sutcliffe, K. M. and Obstfeld, D. 2005. Organizing and the process of sensemaking. *Organization science*, 16(4), pp. 409-421. doi: 10.1287/orsc.1050.0133.

Wenger, E., White, N., Smith, J. and Rowe, K. 2005. Technology for communities. *Working, learning and collaborating in a network: Guide to the implementation and leadership of intentional communities of practice*, 14, pp. 71-94. http://www.technologyforcommunities. com/CEFRIO_Book_Chapter_v_5.2.pdf.

Wenger E. 1998. *Communities of practice: Learning, meaning and identity.* New York, NY: Cambridge University Press.

Young, M. L. and Tseng, F. C. 2008. Interplay between physical and virtual settings for online interpersonal trust formation in knowledge-sharing practice. *Cyberpsychology & Behavior*, 11(1), pp. 55-64. doi: 10.1089/cpb.2007.0019.

In: The Impact of COVID-19 on Teaching ...   ISBN: 978-1-53619-947-5
Editors: S. Studente, S. Ellis et al.   © 2021 Nova Science Publishers, Inc.

Chapter 3

STAYING CONNECTED: MINIMIZING ISOLATION AND BUILDING LEARNING COMMUNITIES VIA CHATBOT TECHNOLOGY

*Sylvie Studente**, *PhD*

Regent's University London, London, United Kingdom

ABSTRACT

The COVID-19 pandemic began at the end of 2019, and the virus is reported to be highly contagious and transmitted through contact with others (Liu et al, 2020). In response to the pandemic, global lockdown measures were introduced on the 20th March 2020 which affected students in 142 countries worldwide (Karalis & Raikou, 2020). Across the global HE landscape, universities closed and were required to move to an online mode of teaching and learning immediately (Bisht et al, 2020). The disruption caused to higher education by the pandemic has had a significant impact on the learning experience for students (Hill & Fitzgerald, 2020). High student engagement with studies, with their lecturers and with other students is reported to be associated with successful learning (Zepke & Leach, 2010; Docherty et al, 2018). When students are not engaged, this can be detrimental to their learning success and lead to feelings of

---

* Corresponding Author's E-mail: sylvie.studente@regents.ac.uk.

disconnect (Bryson, 2014). From a student perspective, self-directed study time has increased (Aucejo et al, 2020), levels of stress and anxiety experienced by students has increased (Karalis & Raikou, 2020), and the lack of face-to-face interaction with lecturers and other students has led to feelings of isolation (Muhammad & Kainat, 2020).

The adoption of chatbot technology within HE is associated with several benefits including improving student motivation, improving student attention, encouraging collaborative learning, promoting communication with peers, and increasing student's sense of ease (Gulz, 2004). Feelings of "social isolation" are reported to be a key cause of low engagement for international students in particular. These feelings can be exacerbated if students receive little opportunity to engage in learning communities to receive peer support (Cross, 1998). In this chapter, the use of chatbot technology is discussed as a solution to establish learning communities to provide students with a sense of connectedness and belonging. This chapter reports upon two studies conducted at a London University with a largely international student base. Specifically, the studies reported within this chapter focus upon creating learning communities with students, programme leaders, and module leaders. This chapter reports on how the chatbot was implemented pre and during lockdown to help students feel more connected, and how the chatbot was incorporated within teaching and learning activities during online modes of delivery.

Keywords: chatbot, learning, learning communities, higher education

1. INTRODUCTION

This chapter reports upon two studies introducing chatbot technology to develop learning communities at a London University, with a largely international student base. The first study, a pilot, was conducted over the autumn term of 2019, the focus was twofold to ease the transition for students into their first year of university study, and to increase study engagement. As part of this study, four learning communities were created using the chatbot at undergraduate and post graduate level. Students and programme leaders were provided with access to the chatbot via mobile app prior to study induction and throughout the autumn term of 2019. At the end of the term, data was collected via questionnaires and focus groups with students and programme leaders to allow for identification of benefits and challenges. Findings indicated a positive correlation between study engagement and engagement with peers. Students reported that the chatbot enabled them to obtain support and connect to their programme leader. Both staff and students also made recommendations on how engagement could be further enhanced using the chatbot in terms of clearly specified purpose, integration with existing university systems, leading by example and connectivity. Extending upon these recommendations, a second study was carried out during the lockdown of 2020. In the second study the focus was upon creating learning communities with students and module leaders. Modules were selected where previous engagement levels had been low. This chapter reports upon how the chatbot was implemented during lockdown to not only help students feel more connected, but also reports upon how the chatbot was incorporated within teaching and learning activities during online modes of delivery.

2. BACKGROUND MOTIVATION

2.1. What Are Chatbots?

A chatbot is defined as an interactive messenger powered by artificial intelligence which enables users to interact via a chat interface (Schlicht, 2016). Chatbots are powered by artificial intelligence and not only enable students to communicate via a chat interface, but they also make use of pattern matching to link students to a "mentor" (Gill, 2019; Desaulniers, 2016). Students are already familiar with mobile chat applications, and chatbots extend upon this concept by providing students with a collaborative environment within which to communicate with each other and ask questions (Singh, 2018). Although there has been a rise in the adoption of chatbots across the HE landscape (Studente, Ellis & Garivaldis, 2020), research in the area is still relatively new (Sandoval, 2018; Gonda et al., 2018), and research within the area is limited (Yang & Evans, 2019).

2.2. Assisting the Transition from School to University Life

The initial focus of the chatbot project reported within this chapter was to assist students with the transition from school to university. A major challenge faced by students when starting university is a feeling of being disconnected from other students and lecturers in amongst finding their way in a new structure and environment (Jones et al., 2009). Increased feelings of isolation and loneliness are generally reported as reasons for poor integration of students into university life (Studente, Ellis & Garivaldis, 2020b). It is reported that these feelings of isolation can be exacerbated if students receive limited opportunities to engage in learning communities within which they could receive peer support (Cross, 1998).

Added to the challenges of transitioning to university, are reported low-engagement and high drop-out rates within the first year of study. Research suggests a link between the provision of individual student support and drop-out rates in higher education, particularly if students feel isolated in the transition from school to university (Peel, 2000; Jones et al., 2009). For some students, the transition from school to university can be overwhelming (Briggs et al., 2012), which can lead to feelings of social disconnect with peers. Feeling connected with other students has been linked to student motivation with studies (Rau et al., 2008). For students who experience feelings of social disconnect, chatbot technology can facilitate the development of relationships with others as well as providing general assistance (Harley et al., 2007). Low engagement leads to a number of detrimental outcomes such as poor results, feelings of isolation and increasing drop-out rates, and is a common challenge to students transitioning from school to university (Hone & El Said, 2016). Chatbots are increasingly being utilised to address engagement in HE institutions in response to this challenge (Studente & Ellis, 2020).

Chatbots are also becoming increasingly popular in HE institutions in solving the challenge of providing individual student support (Winkler & Söllner, 2018). This is particularly important in the context of first year students who may initially feel isolated. In the case of international students, these feelings of isolation may be amplified due to dealing with high levels of cultural adjustment (Erichsen & Bolliger, 2011). A study on cross-cultural adjustment by McClure (2007) identified feelings of social isolation as a challenge for international students. Social isolation is defined as feelings of "loneliness and marginalisation" (Reynolds & Constantine, 2007). Research further purports that students may experience feelings of isolation if they feel they have little opportunity to engage in learning communities and receive peer support (Cross, 1998). Crawford and Cook (2008) assert that learning success is in part determined by developing connections with peers and educators as part of a community. Chatbots have the potential to offer a solution towards not only establishing "communities" but also to support learning in collaborative settings (Tegos et al., 2015). Such an approach offers an innovative way to improve the student learning experience by "tapping-in" to the popularity of the use of mobile phone devices (Arnold, 2018).

2.3. The Impact of the COVID-19 Pandemic

Feelings of disconnectedness and isolation have been exacerbated by global lockdowns as a consequence of the COVID-19 pandemic (Karalis & Raikou, 2020; Bu et al., 2020). The outbreak led to university campuses closing and moving to online modes of teaching and learning with short notice (Bisht et al, 2020; Rahiem, 2020; Wickersham et al., 2021), for many students this has been a disorienting experience (Watermeyer et al., 2021). The shift to remote learning is reported to have resulted in a loss of personal contact for students with peers and tutors (Werner et al., 2021), impeding social interactions which would ordinarily take place during classes (Ilias et al., 2020).

Student engagement has also been impacted (Muhammad & Kainat, 2020). When students are not engaged, this can be detrimental to their learning success and lead to further feelings of disconnect (Bryson, 2014). Within this chapter, the use of chatbot technology is advocated as a solution during these challenging times, to provide students with connectedness and a sense of belonging, both of which are essential to effective learning. Added to these challenges are increased levels of stress, anxiety and depression for students owing to the lockdown (Wang et al., 2020; Kaparounaki et al., 2020; Husky et al., 2020). There are further complexities for international students with many having returned to their home countries amongst the outbreak, and not able to continue their studies aside from online (Fernandez, 2020).

2.4. Chatbots as a Solution

In the context of education chatbots are utilised for numerous purposes including enabling students to acquire information related to academic studies (Heo & Lee, 2019), selection of elective modules (Ho et al., 2018), tutoring (Gonda et al., 2018), reminding students of class timetables and assessment deadlines (Larsson, 2019), providing support for students 24/7 (Gonda et al., 2018; Andriotis, 2017), providing FAQs (Sandoval, 2018), facilitating interactivity and socialbility (AbuShawar & Atwell, 2015), helping students to transition into their first year at university (Carayannopoulos, 2017), and creating learning communities (Lauricella & Kay, 2013).

The adoption of chatbot technology within HE is associated with several benefits including increasing student motivation (Fryer & Carpenter, 2006), improving attention (Song et al., 2017), interaction with peers (Goggins & Xing, 2016), facilitating self-directed learning (Johnson, 2006), developing learning communities (Alencar and Netto, 2011; Cross, 1998), improving student engagement (Pereira, 2016), improving student retention (Benotti et al., 2014), encouraging collaborative learning (Bii, 2013), increasing student satisfaction (Radziwill & Benton, 2017), increasing student confidence (Jia and Chen, 2009), answering student's queries (Feng et al., 2006), functioning as teaching assistants (Pereira, 2016), decreasing demands for low value repetitive work on lecturers (Carayannopoulos, 2017) and increasing student's sense of ease (Gulz, 2004).

2.5. Differ Chatbot

Differ is a chatbot which is a messaging app for students and lecturers in higher education. It is the result of a 5-year long Norwegian R&D project including BI Norwegian Business school and an education technology start-up called Edtech Foundry. Differ is a messaging app for students and educators in HE which uses chatbots to facilitate conversations replacing social media applications such as Facebook groups, WhatsApp, email etc, into one integrated environment. In Differ, chatbots are used to match students to each other to initiate conversations and pair students with peer mentors. Through Differ students can receive responsive information regarding modules of study and support services or use it for social purposes to meet up and connect with new people with similar interests or issues to raise (Differ, 2020). Differ can be downloaded onto mobile phones as well as a desktop application (see Figure 1).

Figure 1. The Differ chatbot via desktop and mobile phone app.

3. STUDY ONE (PILOT)

3.1. Overview

This study was conducted at the "programme level," with programme leaders and students being provided with access to the Differ chatbot. Four learning communities were created level 3 foundation students, level 4 undergraduate students, level 6 undergraduate students and level 7 post-graduate students. Each community area in Differ consisted of an announcements page that programme leaders could use to contact students, an open chat area for each community, and a list of peers enrolled within the community. Using Differ students were able to connect to classmates via one-to-one chat and group chat. Students were also able to connect to their programme leader directly using Differ.

Students were emailed with a link to sign up to Differ to encourage them to connect to their new classmates prior to the start of the new academic term. Then during induction week students and programme leaders were introduced to using the chatbot and were provided with access to Differ throughout the autumn term of 2019. Towards the end of term, qualitative and quantitative data was collected through questionnaires and focus groups.

3.2. Data Collection

Qualitative and quantitative data was collected via questionnaires distributed across all four learning communities to ascertain student opinions on having used the chatbot over the autumn term 2019. The 15-item questionnaire consisted of four key sections demographic information, study programme engagement, use of Differ, and further suggestions regarding the chatbot. A mixture of question types were used to elicit Likert style responses to gauge strength of agreement, for example with student's perceived level of programme engagement, through to open-ended questions regarding perceived benefits of the chatbot. In addition, four focus groups were held with level 4 undergraduate, level 6 undergraduate, level 7 postgraduate and programme leaders. The student focus groups comprised open-ended questions related to engagement with study programme, connectivity with peers, usage of Differ, how students used Differ to connect to others, perceived benefits, and ideas for future development regarding the chatbot. The staff (programme leader) focus group comprised 12 open-ended questions related to student engagement on academic programmes, student engagement through Differ, perceived benefits of the chatbot, perceived challenges, and ideas on future development. All focus groups ran for approximately 40 minutes and were recorded and transcribed.

3.3. Findings

Of the 74 participants who completed the questionnaire, 58% (N = 43) were male, and 42% (N = 31) were female, with ages ranging from 17 years to 31 years ($M = 21$, $SD = 2.655$). Participants differed in the level of education they were receiving. Specifically, 34% (N = 25) of participants were Level 3 Foundation students, 23% (N = 17) were Level 4 undergraduate students, 23% (N = 17) were level 6 undergraduate students, and 20% (N = 15) were level 7 postgraduate students.

Participants reported an overall positive engagement with their studies ($M = 7.89$, $SD = 1.458$) and their classmates ($M = 7.38$, $SD = 2.105$) in general. A Pearson correlation analysis yielded a significantly strong positive correlation between engagement with studies and engagement with classmates ($r (73) = .629$, $p = .000$), such that participants who reported engagement with their studies were very likely to report engagement with their classmates. Similar levels of engagement were experienced across all four learning communities. Participants were asked to report whether Differ enabled them to connect to their programme leader, feel connected in general, and obtain support. The results are displayed in Table 1.

Table 1. Frequency data

	N	To connect to programme leader (N)	To feel more connected (N)	To obtain support (N)
Level 3 Foundation	12	0	0	3
Level 4 undergraduate	3	1	1	2
Level 6 undergraduate	13	9	4	8
Level 7 postgraduate	13	1	0	0

Table 2. Ideas on the future use of Differ

Theme	Comments made
Promoting student-teacher interaction	The app could promote student-teacher interaction and should be used more widely by teachers and the university as a whole. As such, the app could be integrated with other university systems, and other platforms that students already use, such as Blackboard and university emails.
Networking	The app could serve as a networking app, to connect with classmates that students may work with in future.
Additional features	The app could include additional features. For example, it was suggested that Differ include a Q&A feature, whereby students ask the app questions, such as "when are my assignments due?" and the app responds with a list of assignments and deadlines.
User-friendly design	Differ needs to be more user-friendly, like other familiar apps, such as WhatsApp. It was also suggested that Differ should send out notifications, similar to emails and notifications from Blackboard. Currently users are required to go through 3 or 4 steps to find the chat window. It was suggested that the chat is the first thing that should appear as the user opens the app.

Qualitative data was collected from both the questionnaire and focus groups. Participants stated that they felt more comfortable using the chatbot to contact their programme leader rather than email, as this form of communicationfelt more personalized. Participants also stated that using the chatbot helped them to connect with their peers more easily and closely.

Participants also stated that they received support via Differ from their programme leader in understanding assignments better, and in getting a response quicker than via email. Participants were asked about how they see Differ being used in the future, the responses form which are shown in table 2.

Participants were also asked how they believed Differ could be used to enhance engagement. Responses from both the questionnaire and focus groups have been grouped into five themes integration at module level, alignment with coursework requirements, accessibility from the university landing page, improved interaction from lecturers and improvement to group communications. Comments made within these themes are summarised in Table 3.

Table 3. Ideas on improving engagement through Differ

Theme	Comments made
Integration at module level	The use of Differ could be mandatory and used for every module more purposefully.
Alignment with coursework requirements	Differ could be aligned with coursework requirements and assignments, and enable group-work via linked google docs.
Improved interaction from lecturers	There should be more university driven communications through Differ, including by lecturers.
Improvement to group communications	Group forum features could be improved so that students can have more specific and targeted communication with each other based on similar interests, and not just who they already know. This would facilitate across-programme/pathway communication, which is not common in face-to-face.

Drawing on the evidence and participant feedback presented above, recommendations are made for the future use of Differ as outlined in table 4.

The above recommendations were used to re-design elements of the chatbot which was relaunched at a more granular 'module' level as opposed to 'programme' level. A second study followed during the lockdown period in the Spring term of 2020. This is reported on in the following section.

Table 4. Recommendations moving forward with Differ

Recommendation	Explanation
Recommendation one: purpose of the chatbot	Differ currently competes with other apps that students are either already using or are familiar with. The purpose of Differ should be different to the purpose of other apps, such as WhatsApp.
Recommendation two: integration with existing university systems	The need to use Differ, rather than other apps needs to be established. This could be done by expanding the adoption of the app across the institution, and integrating it with existing systems, such as Blackboard and email.
Recommendation three: leading by example	Lecturers and the institution should initiate and facilitate connection and use of the app, leading by example. Lecturers should also be encouraged to refrain from using other platforms, such as Facebook and WhatsApp, to direct students to Differ.
Recommendation four: roll-out	The roll-out of the app needs consideration. The app may be easier to introduce to foundation or level 4 students, who are new to the university and do not have pre-existing modes of communication between them.
Recommendation five: connectivity as the focal point	The chat feature of the app should not be the selling point, as students have other forms of chat. Rather, the selling point should be connectivity with the lecturer and the coursework/content of modules/programmes.
Recommendation six: improvements to usability	The usability of the app could be improved, so that it is more intuitive and easier to use.

4. STUDY TWO

4.1. Overview

The second study was conducted during Autumn 2020 during "lockdown." The focus was upon the "module level" as opposed to the programme level, with module leaders and students being provided access to the Differ chatbot. Four learning communities were created as follows level 3 foundation students, two groups of level 5 undergraduate students, and level 7 post-graduate students.

From the feedback received from study one, additional features were added to the chat bot. This included a "matching" feature which pairs students with peers. This is illustrated in Figure 2.

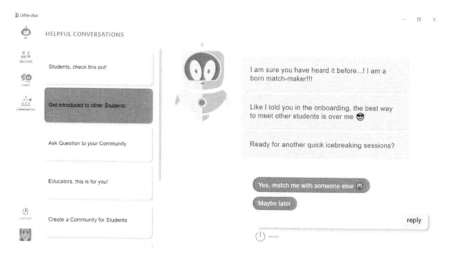

Figure 2. Matching students with peers.

This feature was added in order to allow students to connect with peers and thus assist with reducing feelings of isolation. This was felt of vital importance owing to classes moving to remote delivery during the lockdown period. When asked about additional features students would like to see included in study 1, participants stated that they would like to see a Q & A feature by which they could ask the chatbot questions regarding assessments. It was felt that such a feature would also reduce demands on lecturer's time as students would be able to access a Q & A feature 24/7. For each of the four modules of focus for study two, a Q & A feature was added that was specific to each module (see Figure 3).

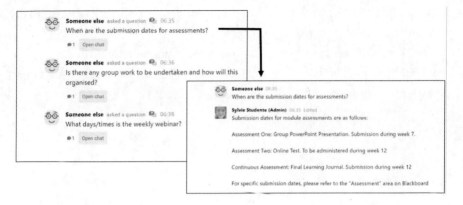

Figure 3. Q&A feature.

4.2. Setting up Learning Communities

As previously mentioned, four learning communities were set up for this study, these modules were selected due to previously low engagement levels and pass rates. Each learning community was set up to include an announcements page that module leaders could use to contact students, an open chat area for each community, and a list of peers enrolled within the community. Using Differ, students were able to connect to classmates via one-to-one chat and group chat. Students were also able to connect to their module leader directly using Differ. A Q & A feature was also included for each learning community. The "announcements" area was used by module leaders to set learning tasks for students, and individual student group areas were created for student-group discussions on weekly learning topics.

As can be seen from Figure 4, this community area consisted of; an announcement area (where the module leader could post announcements to students), an open chat area (where students could post to the whole community), Q & A sections, an ice-breaker section (titled "Say Hi"), and group work areas.

The group areas were set up to assist students with group-work as part of their assessment coursework. As part of their assessment for this module, students were divided into four groups and undertook group discussions within Differ (see Figure 4). The "open chat" area was used to discuss weekly topics covered within online webinar sessions during the academic term (see Figure 5).

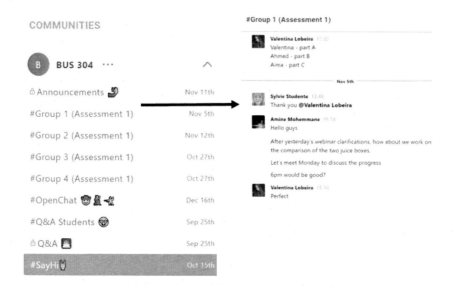

Figure 4. Learning community area for level 3 students.

Figure 5 illustrates the use of the "open chat area" for a discussion on the topic of "accounting" which was covered in a webinar session for the module. Across all four learning communities, the chatbot was used to actively encourage engagement with module studies. Figure 6 illustrates the use of the chatbot to set learning activities across different webinar groups within a module.

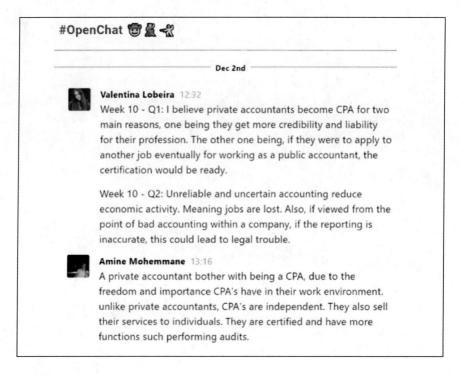

Figure 5. Use of the open chat area for topic discussions.

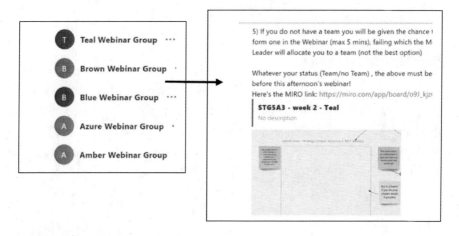

Figure 6. Use of the open chat area for topic discussions.

4.3. Discussion

The additions made to the chatbot during the study conducted during the lockdown period sought to minimise feelings of isolation due to lack of face-to-face interaction. This has been a topic of concern in Higher Education owing to the COVID 19 pandemic (Muhammad & Kainat, 2020). Establishing learning communities is viewed as paramount to successful learning (Tegos et al., 2015), and this is especially true during the pandemic (Karalis & Raikou, 2020). The university where the studies were conducted has a largely international student base, and when the lockdown was first announced, many students returned to their home countries, studying solely online via webinars. To facilitate feelings of connectedness, the matching feature enabled students to be matched with peers (see Figure 2). Through using the chatbot, students could also see profile images of other students enrolled on their module and could send each other chat messages. In establishing the learning communities, students were instantly connected with their peers and their module leader. It was felt that instantly linking students with their peers and module leader would assist in reducing feelings of stress and anxiety reportedly faced by many students as a consequence of the pandemic. Throughout the term students used the chatbot to contact their module leaders as well as peers.

Lack of engagement has also been reported to be a challenge in Higher Education (Bryson, 2014). The additions made to the chatbot in the second study also sought to maximise student engagement with modules. This engagement was driven by module leaders to incorporate the use of the chatbot into webinar groups and assessment work (see Figures 4 and 6). Use of the "open chat" area also facilitated weekly topic discussions between students (see Figure 5). Throughout the term, students used the chatbot to develop webinar and group assessment work. Leading on from recommendations obtained from the pilot study, the chatbot was further developed to provide general assistance to students via a Q & A feature. This enabled students to access information regarding webinar timetables and assessment deadlines instantaneously, whilst reducing demand on lecturers during the lockdown period. Overall, the added features of the chatbot facilitated the development of learning communities by which students could develop important relationships with peers and lecturers, engage with their studies and access information necessary to their studies. It was not possible to collect additional information at the conclusion of the second study due to the ongoing lockdown and physical dispersal of teaching staff and students.

CONCLUSION

In this chapter, the use of chatbots has been advocated as an effective tool for establishing learning communities, providing students with a sense of connectedness, and belonging. The remote approach towards learning owing to the COVID-19 pandemic has reportedly not only exacerbated feelings of isolation but has also led to a decline in student engagement (Bahja et al., 2020). Due to the physical closure of universities as a consequence of the pandemic, there has been an increase in demand for new approaches towards e-learning. It is at a time now more than ever that reliance on technology for social interaction is of utmost importance. This assertion is strongly supported by research which states that the use of chatbots in education assists with developing meaningful interactions between students and lecturers (Goggins & Xing, 2016). It is through facilitating interaction and socialisation that chatbots can help reduce feelings of loneliness (Brandtzaeg & Folstad, 2018; Piccolo et al., 2018).

This chapter has reported upon a number of challenges faced by students as a consequence of the COVID-19 pandemic, chatbots are a potential solution for addressing some of these challenges. It is further recommended that as well as conversational use, chatbots should be used to enhance the learning process in higher education. In the words of Fernoga (2018), chatbots provide the opportunity to act as an *"intelligent bridge"* between technology and education. The benefits of which, can be especially garnered in instances where remote and/or blended learning scenarios are of paramount focus.

REFERENCES

AbuShawar, B. & Atwell, E. (2015). ALICE chatbot: trials and outputs. *Computacion y Sistemas.* 19, 4. Pp 625 – 632. [*Computing and Systems*]

Alencar, M., & Netto, J. (2011). Developing a 3D Conversation Agent Talking About Online Courses. *Proceedings of World Conference on Educational Multimedia, Hypermedia and Telecommunications,* 1713 - 1719.

Andriotis, N. (2017). *Are Chatbots the Next Big Thing in Digital Learning?* Retrieved from https://www.talentlms.com/blog/chatbots-next-big-thing-digital-learning.

Arnold, A. (2018). *How Chatbots Feed into Millennials' Need for Instant Gratification.* Retrieved from https://www.forbes.com/sites/andrew arnold/2018/01/27/how-chatbots-feed-into-millennials-need-for-instant-gratification/#68883d736750.

Aucejo, E., French, J., Paola, M., Araya, U. & Zafar, B. (2020). The impact of COVID-19 on student experiences and expectations: Evidence from a survey. *Journal of Public Economic.* 191. Doi: 104271.

Bahja, M., Hammas, R., & Butt, G. (2020). A user centric framework for educational chatbots design and development. *Proceedings of the International Conference on Human-Computer Interaction.* Pp 32 – 43.

Benotti, L., Martínez, M., & Schapachnik, F. (2014). Engaging High School Students Using Chatbots. *Proceedings of the 2014 conference on Innovation & technology in computer science education,* 63 – 68.

Bii, P. (2013). Chatbot technology: A possible means of unlocking student potential to learn how to learn. *Educational Research,* 4, 2, 218 - 22.

Bisht, R., Jasola, S. & Bisht, I. (2020). Acceptability and challenges of online higher education in the era of COVID-19: a study of student's perspective. *Asian Education and Development Studies.* Doi: https://doi.org/10.1108/AEDS-05-2020-0119.

Brandtzaeg, P. & Folstad, A. (2018). Chatbots: changing user needs and motivations. *Interactions.* Vol. 25, No. 2.

Briggs, A., Clark, J. & Hall, I. (2012). Building bridges: understanding student transition to university. *Quality in Higher Education.* 18, 1. Pp 3 – 21.

Bryson, C. (2014). *Understanding and Developing Student Engagement. Routledge.*

Bu, F., Steptoe, A. & Fancourt, D. (2020). Who is lonely in lockdown? Cross cohort analyses of preditors of loneliness before and during the COVID-19 Pandemic. *Public Health.* Doi: 10.1016/j.puhe.2020.06.036.

Carayannopoulos, S. (2017). Using chatbots to aid transition. *International Journal of Information and Learning Technology.* 35, 2. Pp 118 – 129.

Crawford, C., & Cook, R. (2008). Creating and Sustaining Communities of Learning within Distance Learning Environments: Focusing upon Making Connections, Creating Communities of Learning, and Responsibilities. *International Journal of Learning*, 15, 2, 179 - 193.

Cross, K. (1998). *Why learning communities? Why now? About Campus*, 3, 3, 4 – 11.

Desaulniers, S. (2016). *Chatbots rise, and the future may be 're-written.'* Retrieved from http://www.cnbc.com/2016/04/08/chatbots-rise-and-the-future- may-be-re-written.html.

Differ. (2020). *Help Your Students Succeed.* Retrieved from https:// www.differ.chat

Docherty, A., Warkentin, P., Borgen, J., Garthe, K., Fischer, K. & Najjar, R. (2018). Enhancing student engagement: innovative strategies for intentional learning. *Journal of Professional Nursing.* 34, 6. Pp 470 – 474.

Erichsen, E., & Bolliger, D. (2011). Towards understanding international graduate student isolation in traditional and online environments. *Educational Technology Research and Development*, 59, 309 – 326.

Feng, D., Shaw, E., Kim, J., & Hovy, E. (2006). An intelligent discussion-bot for answering student queries in threaded discussions. *Proceedings of the 11th International Conference on Intelligent User Interfaces*, 171 – 177.

Fernandez, A. (2020). Impact of COVID-19: University Students' Perspective. International Journal of Nutrition, *Pharmacology and Neurological Diseases.* 10, 3. Pp 168 – 169.

Fernoga, V., Stelea, G., Gavrila, C. & Sandu, F. (2018). Intelligent educational assistant powered by chatbots. *Proceedings of the 14th International Scientific Conference on eLearning and Software for Education.* Burcharest.

Fryer, L., & Carpenter, R. (2006). Bots as Language Learning Tools. *Language Learning & Technology*, 10, 3, 8 – 14.

Gill, M (2019). *5 Ways Artificial Intelligence and Chatbots Are Changing Education.* Retrieved from https://towardsdatascience.com/5-ways-artificial-intelligence-and-chatbots-are-changing-education-9e7d9425421d.

Goggins, S., & Xing, W. (2016). *Building models explaining student participation behavior in asynchronous online discussion.* Computers & Education, 94, 241 - 251.

Gonda, D., Lei, C., Chai, Y., Hou, X. & Tam, V. (2018). Chatbot tutors for blended learning: why bother? And where to start? *Proceedings of the International Conference on Teaching, Assessment and Learning for Engineering.* Wollongong, Australia.

Gulz, A. (2004). Benefits of Virtual Characters in Computer Based Learning Environments: Claims and Evidence. *International Journal of Artificial Intelligence in Education*, 14, 3, 313 – 334.

Harley, D., Winn, S., Pemberton, S. & Wilcox, P. (2007). Using texting to support student's transition to university. *Innovations in Education and Teaching International.* 44, 3. Pp 229 – 241.

Heo, J. & Lee, J. (2019). An inclusive chatbot service for international students and academics. *Proceedings of the International Conference on Human Computer Interaction.* Pp 153 – 167.

Hill, K. & Fitzgerald, R. (2020). Student perspectives of the impact of COVID-19 on learning. *All Ireland Journal of Higher Education.* 12, 2. Pp 1 – 9.

Ho, C., Lee, H., Lo, W., Lui, K. (2018). Developing a chatbot for college student programme advisement. *Proceedings of the International Symposium on Educational Technology.*

Hone, K., & El Said, G. (2016). Exploring the factors affecting MOOC retention: A survey study. *Computers & Education*, 98. Pp 157 – 168.

Husky, M., Kovess-Masfety, V. & Swendsen, J. (2020). Stress and anxiety among university students in France during COVID-19 mandatory confinement. *Comprehensive Psychiatry.* 102. 152191.

Ilias, A., Baidi, N., Ghani, E., Razali, F. (2020). Issues on the Use of Online Learning: An Exploratory Study Among University Students During the COVID-19 Pandemic. *Universal Journal of Educational Research.* 8, 11. Pp 5092 - 5105.

Jia, J., & Chen, W. (2009). Motivate the Learners to Practice English through Playing with Chatbot CSIEC. *Proceedings of the 3rd international conference on Technologies for E-Learning and Digital Entertainment*, 180 - 191.

Johnson, G. (2006). Synchronous and asynchronous text-based CMC in educational contexts: A review of recent research. *TechTrends*, 50, 4, 46 – 53.

Jones, G., Edwards, G. & Reid, A. (2009). How can mobile SMS communication support and enhance a first-year undergraduate learning environment? *Research in Learning Technology.* 17, 3. Pp 201 – 218.

Kaparounaki, C., Patsali, M., Mousa, D., Papadopoulou, V., Papadopoulou, K. & Fountoulakis, K. (2020). University students' mental health amidst the COVID-19 quarantine in Greece. *Psychiatry Research.* 290. 113111.

Karalis, T. & Raikou, N. (2020). Teaching at the times of COVID-19: Inferences and implications for higher education pedagogy. *International Journal of Academic Research in Business and Social Sciences.* 10, 5. Pp 479 – 493.

Lauricella, S. & Kay, R. (2013). Investigating and comparing communication media used in higher education. *Journal of Communication Technology and Human Behaviours.* 2, 1. Pp 1 – 20.

Liu, Y., Kuo, R. & Shih, S. (2020). COVID-19: The first documented coronavirus pandemic in history. *Biomedical Journal*. 43, 4. Pp 328 – 333.

McClure, J. (2007). International graduates' cross-cultural adjustment: Experiences, coping strategies, and suggested programmatic responses. *Teaching in Higher Education*, 12, 2. Pp 199 – 217.

Muhammad, A. & Kainat, A. (2020). Online learning amid the COVID-19 pandemic: student's perspectives. *Journal of Pedagogical Sociology and Psychology*. 2, 1. Pp 45 – 51.

Peel, M. (2000). 'Nobody cares:' the challenge of isolation in school to university transition. *Journal of Institutional Research*, 22 - 34.

Pereira, J. (2016). Leveraging chatbots to improve self-guided learning through conversational quizzes. *Proceedings of the 4th International Conference on Technological Ecosystems for Enhancing Multiculturality*, 911 – 918.

Piccolo, L., Mensio, M. & Alani, H. (2018). Chasing the chatbots. *Proceedings of the International Conference on Internet Science*. Pp 157 – 169.

Radziwill, N., & Benton, M. (2017). Evaluating Quality of Chatbots and Intelligent Conversational Agents. *Computers and Society*.

Rahiem, M. (2020). The emergency remote learning experience of university students in Indonesia amidst the COVID-19 crisis. *International Journal of Learning, Teaching and Educational Research*. 19, 6. Pp 1 – 26.

Rau, P., Gao, Q. & Wu, L. (2008). Exploring the use of text and instant messaging in higher education classrooms. *Research in Learning Technology*. 21, 1. Pp 1 – 17.

Reynolds, A., & Constantine, M. (2007). Cultural adjustment difficulties and career development of international college students. *Journal of Career Assessment*, 15, 3. Pp 338 – 350.

Sandoval, Z. (2018). Design and implementation of a chatbot in online higher education settings. *Issues in Information Systems*. 19, 4. Pp 44 – 55.

Schlicht, M. (2016). *The Complete Beginner's Guide to Chatbots*. Retrieved from https://chatbotsmagazine.com/the-complete-beginner-s guide-to-chatbots-8280b7b906ca#.5vs9cl5ut.

Singh, R. (2018). *AI and Chatbots in Education: What Does the Future Hold?* Retrieved from https://chatbotsmagazine.com/ai-and-chatbots-in-education-what-does-the-futurehold-9772f5c13960.

Song, D., Rice, M., & Young Oh, E. (2019). Participation in Online Courses and Interaction with a Virtual Agent. *International Review of Research in Open and Distributed Learning*. 20, 1. Pp 249 – 257.

Studente, S. & Ellis, S. (2020). Enhancing the Online Student Experience Through Creating Learning Communities: The Benefits of Chatbots in Higher Education. In S. McKenzie, M. Mundy, F. Garivaldis & K. Dyer (Eds.) *Tertiary Online Teaching and Learning: TOTAL Perspectives and Resources for Digital Education*. Springer-Verlag.

Studente, S., Ellis, S. & Garivaldis, F. (2020). The impact of chatbots to pedagogy and student engagement: preliminary findings and lessons from a pilot. In R. Nata (Ed.) *Progress in Education*. Nova Science Publishers.

Studente, S., Ellis, S. & Garivaldis, F. (2020b). Exploring the Potential of Chatbots in Higher Education: A Preliminary Study. *International Conference on Advanced Learning Technologies*. Amsterdam.

Tegos, S., Stavros, D., & Karakostas, A. (2015). Promoting academically productive talk with conversational agent interventions in collaborative learning settings. *Computers and Education*, 87, 309 – 325.

Wang, Y., Di, Y., Ye, J. & Wei, W. (2020). Study on the public psychological states and its related factors during the outbreak of coronavirus disease 2019 (COVID-19) in some regions of China. *Psycholgical Health Medicine*. 30. Pp 1 – 10.

Watermeyer, R., Crick, T., Knight, C. & Goodall, J. (2021). COVID-19 and digital disruption in UK universities: afflictions and affordances of emergency online migration. *Higher Education*. 81. Pp 623 – 641.

Werner, A., Tibubos, A., Mulder, L., Reichel, J., Schafer, M., Heller, S., Pfirrmann, D., Edelmann, D., Dietz, P., Rigotti, T., Beutel, M. (2021). *The impact of lockdown stress and loneliness during the COVID-19* pandemic on mental health among university students in Germany. https://doi.org/10.31234/osf.io/9s54k.

Wickersham, A., Carr, E., Hunt, R., Davis, J., Hotopf, M., Fear, N., Downs, J. & Leightley, D. (2021). Changes in physical activity among United Kingdom university students following the implementation of Coronavirus lockdown measures. *International Journal of Environmental Research and Public Health.* 18, 6. Pp 2792.

Winkler, R., & Söllner, M. (2018). *Unleashing the Potential of Chatbots in Education: A State-Of-The-Art Analysis.* Academy of Management Annual Meeting. Chicago, USA.

Yang, S. & Evans, C. (2019). Opportunities and challenges in using AI chatbots in Higher Education. *Proceedings of the 3rd International Conference on Education and E-Learning.* Pp 79 – 83.

Zepke, N. & Leach, L. (2010). Improving student engagement: ten proposals for action. *Active Learning in Higher Education.* 11, 3. Pp 167 – 177.

In: The Impact of COVID-19 on Teaching ...   ISBN: 978-1-53619-947-5
Editors: S. Studente, S. Ellis et al.   © 2021 Nova Science Publishers, Inc.

Chapter 4

DESIGNING AND DELIVERING ONLINE EDUCATION: ONE SIZE DOES NOT FIT ALL

Filia Garivaldis, PhD, Mark Boulet, Bowen Yang
and Sarah Kneebone, PhD
Monash Sustainable Development Institute,
Monash University, Victoria, Australia

ABSTRACT

The global online education sector was expected to become mainstream by 2025. However, the COVID-19 global health crisis has accelerated the adoption of online or flexible modes of teaching and learning. The crisis has also created an unprecedented context for teaching and learning, which has had further impact on how online education has been delivered and received. Despite this upheaval, the higher education industry now has an abundance of experience to draw on, including knowledge of what worked well and what needs to improve in the delivery of education online. In this chapter, we draw on the experience of educators developing and delivering Masters level programs in behaviour change during 2020, in two different case studies. The first case study discussed involves the experience of translating an on-campus unit of study originally designed for face to face delivery, into the fully online mode in response to the Australian government's first imposed "lockdown" restrictions. The second case study presented here involves the building of a purposely designed fully online micro-credential. In both cases, we reflect on the key principles and priorities considered in developing and delivering these programs, and we share some of the feedback received from students on their perceptions of how teaching took place. To conclude, we summarise our reflections on good practice in educational design, that apply irrespective of delivery mode.

Keywords: online education, education principles, purposeful design

INTRODUCTION

As the COVID-19 pandemic hit the higher education sector in early 2020, Universities across the world had little choice but to convert practically all face to face courses of study to the online mode in a bid to retain students and staff, and continue to deliver their educational agenda as smoothly as possible. Academics had suddenly acquired the enormous task of having to translate what they had designed and perfected over the years to deliver to their students in lecture theatres, into a new, and for many, unknown environment; the online learning environment. The differences between face to face and online modes of learning are many and diverse, and issues of feasibility, practicality, and capacity were rife. In some countries, such as developed countries, the transition to online forms of education has been difficult but successful, whilst in other countries the transition has severely exacerbated inequality (Saeed, 2020).

The majority of the units or courses translated to online delivery adopt a process of retrofitting (Kenzig, 2015; Salmons, 2020). This process involves adapting, top down, existing learning materials and resources to a new delivery mode. The aim of retaining as much of the original structure and foundation of the course as possible during this process is partly due to the need to comply with academic calendars and timetables, and in the case of the year 2020, the hope of returning back to 'normal' soon. For some courses, this has meant developing pre-recorded lectures or delivering lectures in real-time through teleconferencing software, adding practice quizzes or discussion forums for students' self-paced asynchronous engagement, or replacing in-class group-based flipchart activities with collaborative synchronous work using Google Docs/Slides. In any of these cases, the retrofitting process involves supplanting instructor-led learning with some student-centred activities through planned intercommunications, interactivity, and collaborations between learners (Payne, 2010; Hai-Jew, 2010) or in-class discussion activities with out-of-class self-paced learning. For other courses, the process of translation involved much more.

At MSDI, and at Monash University more broadly, developing digital education was a key priority since before the pandemic. The Institute was already equipped with the digital learning and video production expertise needed to facilitate both the new demands on its existing face to face education portfolio, alongside pre-existing plans to develop a digital education portfolio. In the following section, we describe two behaviour change programs of study developed by BehaviourWorks Australia (BWA), a specialist behavioural science enterprise within the Monash Sustainable Development Institute (MSDI), and the efforts of BWA teaching staff to deliver these programs in the online mode in 2020. Firstly, we discuss a case of converting to online an on-campus Masters unit on behaviour change, and secondly, we discuss a case of purposefully designing for online a professional development unit on behaviour change.

CASE STUDY ONE: CONVERTING TO ONLINE

ENS5520: Understanding Human Behaviour to Influence Change, was one of the first postgraduate units in Australia that explores the drivers of human behaviour and considers their application to tackling sustainability challenges. An elective six-credit unit in the Leadership specialisation of the Monash Masters of Environment and Sustainability (MES) since 2017, ENS5520 continues to be coordinated and taught by BWA educators and researchers. The unit attracts a diverse range of learners. Some come straight from undergraduate study whilst others have returned to university after some time in the workforce. A number of students work part time in various professions while studying part-time as well.

A typical cohort is usually equally divided into domestic students and international students from Europe, central and eastern Asia and South America. While students from the MES course make up the bulk of enrolments, the unit also attracts others from a variety of Monash postgraduate degrees, including Masters courses in Strategic Communication Management, Project Management, International Development Practice, Public Policy, and Supply Chain Management. In addition, there are usually 1-2 students from external universities, as well as single-unit enrolments from people in industry interested only in this unit. In 2020, the unit welcomed 79 students; the largest cohort since the unit's inception.

The successful conversion of this unit in 2020 to the online mode, in response to COVID-19, was underpinned by two teaching and learning approaches that were foundational to the unit since its first development: Firstly, the unit content gives emphasis to constructive alignment and a flipped classroom approach. The learning material, classroom activities, and assignments of ENS5520 are all tightly woven together and organised such that each week online resources provide the relevant information about a particular topic area, and students apply these to particular scenarios in synchronous classes, which in turn contribute to the progression of assignments. This alignment is based on a flipped classroom model, in which students engage with content online before coming to class. In this model, while classes recap some content, their main focus is the application of this information through activities and groupwork. Content acquisition therefore comes at the student's own pace and they 'lock-in' learning by applying and contextualizing this content when they come together (Lage et al, 2000).

Constructive alignment was crucial to support remote learning in 2020, as students needed to 'self-guide' more than usual. A clear pathway on how to do this was very influential to their successful learning. The use of the flipped classroom approach prior to COVID-19 meant that much of the content was already online for students to access. Our task was, therefore, focused on changing the classroom format to an online version, while still keeping its applied, activity-based, focus. Furthermore, constructive alignment extended beyond the weekly online class activities, into assignments, which had a positive impact on students:

> "I really appreciate how each week the content and tasks are associated to assignments. This is the first unit where the weekly content really relates to assessments and makes our lives so much easier!" (2020, ENS5520 student)

Secondly, the unit gives emphasis to interaction and participatory teaching. Students are motivated to learn by doing and talking together, rather than just listening passively (Mezirow, 1997). Participatory and interactive forms of teaching and learning have been prioritised in ENS5520 since the beginning. These forms of teaching and learning range from hypothetical problem-solving activities to discussion-based presentations that draw on students themselves to help explain new content, and Moodle forums in which students respond to set questions. The focus is often to get students to complete an activity or exercise first and then tease out the key lessons learnt together as a group.

Postgraduate students have rich experience and knowledge from previous study and work, and interactive teaching practices allow them to incorporate what is taught with their existing frames of reference (Mezirow, 1997). They appreciate that teachers are interested in their ideas and experience, and this further motivates learning. Lastly, students provide an excellent source of learning from each other, something which is best achieved when they work together in teams or are called on to share what they think, or have done. This learner-centred approach was kept at the heart of our response to COVID-19 in 2020 and enabled a quick transition to remote learning that was inclusive and supportive of students.

> "Thank you for checking in with me...I have never received a personal-checking-in email from a lecturer before, so I am thrilled to get one from you" (2020 ENS5520 student)

In response to the rapidly implemented campus shut-down in semester 1 2020, a number of rapid changes were made to the unit:

Change 1: Weekly Learning Content Was Captured in Pre-Recorded Videos

COVID-19 was not only a problem of universities, but a problem for all of society, on a global scale. Therefore, flexibility in how teaching and learning was to take place, took precedence. With the help of the BWA communications team, weekly teaching videos were recorded to replace weekly synchronous content delivery, ordinarily covered during the on-campus classes. Our concern was that using online platforms such as Zoom to teach lecture-style material would cause students to lose focus and switch off. Videos were, therefore, seen as a more appropriate way for students to engage with this material in their own time, in light of the challenges and upheavals from lock-down that they, too, were navigating.

An interactive element was retained in these videos by including a number of learning activities that required students to pause the video and read a paper, complete an activity or respond to questions. Students captured activity outcomes in a single weekly Moodle post, which the teaching team read and responded to. The activities were the equivalent of what would have been asked of students in the physical classroom, giving them a chance to consolidate their learnings, and apply them to the assignments.

> "I really enjoy the video lectures/components. I look forward to them after doing the readings as it makes things clearer and engages me more. Pausing the video to reflect/work on questions is also great …I think you're doing well transferring to an online format!" (2020 ENS5520 student)

Change 2: Zoom Classes Were Kept Simple and Aimed to Support Students

As already mentioned, we avoided the temptation to simply replicating what was typically done in the on-campus classroom to a Zoom format. We were also concerned that drawing on the large range of online group-collaboration formats available via Zoom would complicate the learning experience for students and might overwhelm them during an already difficult time. Zoom sessions were, therefore, initially focused on coming together as a cohort and allowing students to meet the teaching team, ask questions about the content and assignments, and meet in break-out groups to share progress on assignments. As students became more comfortable with the Zoom format, we extended the focus of the sessions to include group work that focused on specific activities.

> "Thank you for making this class interesting and fun in spite of it being online. I have really enjoyed the e-lectures and the zoom classes gave me something to look forward to during this quarantine time" (2020 ENS5520 student)

Change 3: Regular Personal Check-Ins with Students

While ENS55220 has always had regular check-ins with students to monitor their progress, this was always a relatively informal process that took the form of discussions with the whole cohort or individual students during class. In 2020, we formalised this approach with a number of repeated activities that allowed us to collect information from students to help us teach better (Black & William, 2009). For instance, the weekly student Moodle posts in response to the video-based activities became a mandatory component of the course and were added to the unit's attendance and participation requirement. The teaching team would review the posts and respond to each one, which proved invaluable in monitoring student progress and challenges experienced with the content. The themes and questions that emerged from these then helped structure the Zoom class discussions.

We also checked in by email with each student personally three times during the semester to see how they were faring with the challenges of lockdown and remote learning, and to get their feedback on how we might continue to improve our online teaching. Here, the focus was not so much to monitor content acquisition and understanding, but simply to provide pastoral care. Our belief is that learner-centred teaching should not just be about supporting knowledge acquisition, but rather about supporting the whole student, akin to walking beside them during a very challenging semester. In our experience, confused and isolated students don't tend to learn well.

> "Thank you again for these check-ins, they have been super helpful in keeping me accountable for weekly classwork" (2020 ENS5520 student)

Unit Outcomes

In addition to the positive feedback that students gave throughout the semester (examples of which are featured throughout this section), ENS5520 received the highest overall student evaluation scores since its inception. The median response to 'overall satisfaction' measures was 4.89 out of 5, placing it in the top 7% of all units (over 1,000) taught across Monash University in semester 1. Of the 79 students that commenced the semester in 2020, all but one successfully completed all assignments.

> "I've thoroughly enjoyed the class and I think you've done a tremendous job in keeping the course interactive despite the forced remote nature! The topics we've covered over the last number of months have already begun to shape some of my work..." (2020 ENS5520 student)

> "Thank you so much for your email. And thank you so much for all your hard work (and your team's) and considerations during these stressful times. I was looking forward to this semester because of this class, and it sure did not disappoint! It's been my absolute favourite so far and I think it should be a must for all specialisations." (2020 ENS5520 student)

CASE STUDY TWO: DESIGNING FOR ONLINE

To enable the content of behavioural science and behaviour change to be accessible to working professionals, an 8 week fully online self-paced version of ENS5520 was developed, in the form of a micro-credential. Although definitions of micro-credentials may vary, at Monash University it is considered a stand-alone short course that enables upskilling in a particular area of practice, which can also provide credit points towards an existing award course. Micro-credentials have become increasingly popular in Australia as working professionals are looking for professional development opportunities that can be put towards additional qualifications. In the case of the micro-credential discussed here, called Applying Behavioural Science to Create Change, six credit points are awarded to learners who successfully complete the assessment requirements of the course—meeting equivalence to ENS5520 in the Master of Environment and Sustainability program, and contributing towards two other Graduate Certificates, to date.

Based on the experience in online education of the course developers and authors of this chapter, in consultation of research evidence of best practice, and based on learner demographics described below (professionals working in government, NGOs, and other private and public organisations), the following priority areas were considered in developing the micro-credential in a purposefully designed online format, each of which present a balance that needs to be maintained for full impact.

Priority 1: Easy Self-Guiding Navigation Within a Clear Structure

Research evidence and feedback obtained directly from students shows that engagement and course completion are compromised when students are unsure how to learn best, and when they struggle to locate learning material in online learning management systems (Broadbent & Lodge, 2020). Several key considerations were applied in designing the structure and navigation of our micro-credential for maximum engagement, the first of which involved meeting the needs and demographic idiosyncrasies of the learners. Specifically, the learners studying the micro-credential make up working professionals, in their majority, with mixed backgrounds. Learners have told us that they registered for the course either to upskill in behavioural science, or to improve their existing use of behavioural insights to better apply evidence-based and theory-informed behaviour change principles and practices in their work. Most learners work on a full time or part time basis, and are several years out of tertiary study practice. Moreover, learners are balancing their studies with competing work and family demands. For all these reasons, it was of paramount importance that the course provided learners with easy access and independent navigation of learning material, to suit multiple backgrounds and preferences.

The course has, therefore, been designed as self-paced, meaning that it can be completed by students flexibly, at a pace (as fast or as slow), and in an order that suits them. This structure plays to the strengths of web-based online learning environments, which have the functionality to offer multiple non-linear navigation options (Scheiter & Gerjets, 2007). In fact, the application of navigation pathways sets purposely designed educational experiences apart from those that use learning management systems as file repositories, or in accordance with the usual face-to-face ordering of content (which requires linearity; Farag & Shemy, 2011). Instead, the learning content of the micro-credential is organised in 8 "modules" rather than "weeks", and uses references to calendar dates only with regard to assessment deadlines. The modules are numbered to provide a recommended sequence for students to complete them in, and grouped into two parts, with "Part 1 - Understanding Behaviour" available to learners on the first day of the course, and "Part 2 - Creating Behaviour Change" before the midway mark. This structure allows for linear navigation for learners who are new to the content and have no prior knowledge, as well as a non-linear navigation for learners who have some experience and are more interested in filling gaps in knowledge (Farag & Shemy, 2011; Rezende & Barros, 2008). In addition to the 8 modules of content is a "Getting started" module, and a "Wrapping up" module, both of which intend to orient students in and out of the course.

> "(I have enjoyed) interesting subject material in bite size amounts. Can work through modules at various times during the week." (2020, micro-credential student)

To assist further with navigation ease, each module of the course comprises 6 to 8 hours of learning consistently, and across the same types of learning assets. That is, each module comprises an interactive eBook, a discussion forum, a quiz, and a downloadable handout, called a "fact sheet". Maintaining consistency across all modules in this way enables learners to establish accurate learning expectations during the course, as well as to apply accurate planning and organisation of time; both of which are critical factors in course completion and performance (Roddy et al., 2017). Each of the learning assets are discussed in further detail in Priority 3, below.

Priority 2: Course Flexibility with Instructor Presence

The flexible nature of online study is what makes this option to upskill and retrain so popular (Allen & Seaman, 2017). Studying flexibly involves a different and more creative use of time, that accommodates the needs of different types of individual learners, such as working professionals, parents and carers, learners of a mature age, and from diverse backgrounds and locations. However, with increased flexibility come additional complications, including feelings of isolation during learning, and reduced prioritisation and planning of learning (Muilenburg & Berge, 2005).

To address these potential problems, the micro-credential was delivered with strong instructor presence in the form of synchronous and asynchronous support. Synchronous activities took the form of online "Meet Ups", or classes that enabled a learner-learner and learner-instructor communication channel in real-time. Participation was voluntary during these events, and learners who could not attend could watch a recording. Those who could and did attend, however, were able to engage with each other and share experiences of the course and their work, have their questions and concerns addressed by experts in the field, and have their needs, either predicted or emergent, addressed effectively (Cowie & Khoo, 2018). Communication and interaction in real time lifts some of the demand of learning from the individual student (Bolliger & Martindale, 2004), and contributes to the multi-modal delivery of content, discussed below. Finally, the option to opt out of attending these meetings increases the chance that learners who did attend did so intrinsically.

"(I have found valuable) the range of experts to learn from, and the ability to study online. I'm busy working with two young children, so I need to fit my studies in around these priorities." (2020, micro-credential student)

Priority 3: Multi-Modal Learning Material

Multi-modal learning has been found to assist students with their comprehension and retention of the learning material (Sankey, Birch, & Gardiner, 2010), enhance experiential learning (Gilakjani, Ismail, & Ahmadi, 2011) and align with the principles of Universal Design for Learning (Rose & Gravel, 2010). Multi-modal representation of content in an enhanced online environment may include any combination of videos and audio elements, recorded lectures, interactive diagrams and simulations, interactive quizzes and graphics (Sankey et al, 2010), and even highly immersive learning environments such as Virtual Reality (VR) (Philippe et al, 2020).

In the micro-credential, multiple modes of content delivery are purposely embedded within eBooks (an online workbook of interactive learning material built in H5P). The eBooks were designed to create meaningful learning environments that do not require students, most of whom are time poor and juggling competing demands, to 'figure things out.' The eBooks are all-inclusive and comprehensive, and contain the readings, videos, and activities learners need to complete in each module. Furthermore, the eBooks contain a narrative that binds the learning material together, and provides "learners with an understanding of what has to be done, how it has to be done, why it has to be done, and when learning goals have been reached" (Starr-Glass, 2018, p. 253).

Whilst the detailed eBooks enabled students to achieve depth and breadth, the most highly rated learning assets of the course are the downloadable fact sheets. The fact sheets are module summaries, created as infographics, that consolidate the key learnings and tools covered in the course. The intention of the fact sheets was to provide engaging and applicable take-away content that would encourage learners to apply their new learning directly to their work.

> "(I have enjoyed) the variety of learning methods - video, research papers, articles - as well as the diverse academics, from some of Monash's professors to other universities who have expertise in the field of behavioural science. To me, this is really important." (2020, micro-credential student)

> "I really enjoyed the diverse learning materials, I think together, they work extremely well. I enjoyed the personalised aspect of watching the academics presenting material, and I enjoyed the animations, podcasts. I also appreciated the grey literature links, which are sometimes a little less daunting than a longer academic article. It was a good mix." (2020, micro-credential student)

> "(I have found valuable) learning the theory and then being asked to apply it to real-world scenarios, even just simple personal examples, in order to demonstrate understanding." (2020, micro-credential student)

Micro-Credential Outcomes

The micro-credential has been delivered several times since its launch in 2020, and consistently receives high student satisfaction scores. The average 'overall satisfaction' score of the course has been 4.51 out of 5, to date. Whilst there is no equivalent course to compare to, other than ENS5520, the micro-credential is promoted within the Institute as a flagship online short course, and has a course completion rate of 78%, which is exemplary for a course of this format.

REFLECTIONS AND CONCLUSIONS

Upon reflection on the processes we adopted in course development, which we engaged in for the purposes of writing this chapter, it became clear that certain themes were common to both cases discussed. These themes include a focus on both the learner and the content, and maintaining a balance between the two, as well as a focus on keeping it simple. Each of these themes are discussed here:

1. Arising from both cases of online course development discussed above, is the focus on the learner. Effective education puts the students or learners at the centre of the learning experience (Bhagat, 2016; Money & Dean, 2019). What we mean by this is that learners and their needs are considered early on in the design of an educational experience, and are subsequently actively engaged during this experience (Hoidn, 2017). Unfortunately, "what learners want" is a question not often addressed in the myriad of guidelines and tools created to assist in online education development. More emphasis is given, although rightly so, to the effective use of technology and multimedia resources, methods for achieving coherence and contiguity within and across different modalities, and others. A good understanding of who the learners are and the context in which they are learning is what we believe to be another critical step in both course design and delivery. Student academic support and pastoral care are both integral to online study success (Roddy et al, 2017).

2. Another theme that arose during our reflection on course development involved maintaining the variety of content and its constructive alignment. We are fortunate to work with subject matter that has a rich professional and personal application, considers both theory and personal experience, and focuses on both the big picture and systems and, simultaneously, narrows in on individual behaviour. Delivering learning content in multiple modalities meant that we were playing to the diversity of learning preferences in our student cohorts, and by constructively aligning all learning activities, we were ensuring that our teaching and learning practices addressed learning goals with coherence (Ruge, Tokede, & Tivendale, 2019).

3. In both cases above, we needed to keep content in moderation, to meet the needs of a diverse range of students. We balanced the

extent to which the content could be completed linearly vs non-linearly to accommodate learners with existing knowledge as well as learners new to the subject area, we balanced the extent to which there was flexibility with a self-paced nature, and accommodated for potential isolation and disengagement along the way with strong instructor presence and pastoral care. We balanced the use material in the course, adopting multiple modes to meet learners' mixed cognitive styles, with never too much reading or too much watching, and never too much learning independently. Online education attracts a greater diversity of students, so addressing this diversity helps circumvent the unintentional consequence of inequality.

4. Keep it simple! The plethora of online collaborative and education focussed platforms available to the teacher can lead to the temptation to 'stuff' an online unit with all sorts of bells and whistles. Yet these run the risk of alienating the learner, especially if they cannot access or use the platforms. Our attention as educators should be on the students, not on the need to impress them with different online tools and platforms.

References

Bhagat, Kaushal. K., Leon Y. Wu, & Chun-Yen C. Y. Chang. 2016. Development and Validation of the Perception of Students Towards Online Learning (POSTOL). *Educational Technology & Society* 19 (1) : 350–359.

Bolliger, Doris. U., & Trey Martindale. 2004. Key factors for determining student satisfaction in online courses. *International Journal of E-Learning* 6: 61–67.

Cowie, Bronwen. & Elaine Khoo. 2018. Tracing Online Lecturer Orchestration of Multiple Roles and Scaffolds Over Time. In *Online Course Management: Concepts, Methodologies, Tools and Applications* edited by Information Resources Management Association's, 258-275. USA: IGI Global.

Ewert, Benjamin. 2020. Moving beyond the obsession with nudging individual behaviour: Towards a broader understanding of Behavioural Public Policy. *Public Policy and Administration* 35 (3) : 337–360.

Farag, Mohammed, & Nader Shemy. 2011. Course Delivery through the Web: Effects of Linear/Nonlinear Navigation and Individual Differences in Online Learning. *International Journal on E-Learning 10* (3) : 243-271.

Gilakjani, Abbas Pourhosein, Hairul N. Ismail, & Seyedeh M. Ahmadi. 2011. The Effect of Multimodal Learning Models on Language Teaching and Learning, *Theory and Practice in Language Studies* 1 (10) : 1321-1327.

Hai-Jew, Shalin. 2010. *An Instructional Design Approach to Updating an Online Course Curriculum*, Accessed April 16, 2021, https://er.educause.edu/articles/2010/12/an-instructional-design-approach-to-updating-an-online-course-curriculum.

Hoidn, Sabine. 2017. *Student-Centered Learning Environments in Higher Education Classrooms*. Palgrave McMillan: Switzerland.

Kenzig, Melissa J. 2015. Lost in Translation: Adapting a Face-to-Face Course Into an Online Learning Experience. *Health Promotion Practice* 16 (5): 625-628.

Lage, Maureen J., Glenn J. Platt, & Michael Treglia. 2000. Inverting the classroom: A gateway to creating an inclusive learning environment. *Journal of Economic Education* 31 (1): 30-43.

Money, William, & Benjamin P. Dean. 2019. Incorporating student population differences for effective online education: A content-based review and integrative model, *Computers & Education* 138 : 57-82.

Muilenburg, Lin. Y., & Zane L. Berge. 2005. Student barriers to online learning: a factor analytic study. *Distance Education* 26 : 29–48.

Payne, Carla R. 2010. *Information Technology and Constructivism in Higher Education: Progressive Learning Frameworks*. Hershey, PA: Information Science Reference.

Peimani, Nastaran, & Hesam Kamalipour. 2021. Online Education and the COVID-19 Outbreak: A Case Study of Online Teaching during Lockdown. *Education Sciences* 11: 72.

Rezende, Flavia. & Susana de Souza Barros. 2008. Students' navigation patterns in the interaction with a mechanics hypermedia program. *Computers & Education* 50: 1370-1382.

Philippe, Stephanie, Alexis D. Souchet, Petros Lameras, Panagiotis Petridis, Julien Caporal, Gildas Coldeboeuf, & Hadrien Duzan. 2020. Multimodal teaching, learning and training in virtual reality: a review and case study, *Virtual Reality & Intelligent Hardware* 2 (5): 421-442.

Roddy, Chantal., Danielle L. Amiet, Jennifer Chung, Christopher Holt, Lauren Shaw, Stephen McKenzie, Filia Garivaldis, Jason M. Lodge & Matthew E. Mundy. 2017. Applying best practice online learning, teaching and support to intensive online environments: An integrative review. *Frontiers in Education* 2: Article 59.

Rose, David .H. & Jenna W. Gravel. 2010. Universal design for learning. In *International Encyclopedia of Education* edited by Eva Baker, Penelope Peterson, & Barry McGaw. Oxford: Elsevier.

Ruge, Gesa, Olubukola Tokede, & Linda Tivendale. 2019. Implementing constructive alignment in higher education – cross-institutional perspectives from Australia, *Higher Education Research & Development* 38 (4): 833-848.

Saeed, Sameerah. 2020. *COVID-19 Has Exacerbated Inequality in Higher Education*. University World News, 24 October 2020.

Salmons, Janet. 2020. *Making a Sudden Transition to Teaching Online: Suggestions and Resources*. Accessed April 9, 2021. https://www.socialsciencespace.com/2020/03/making-a-sudden-transition-to-teaching-online:-suggestions-and-resources/.

Sankey, Michael, Dawn Birch, & Michael Gardiner. 2010. Engaging students through multimodal learning environments: The journey continues. In *Curriculum, technology & transformation for an unknown future* edited by Caroline H. Steel, Mike J. Keppell, Philippa Gerbic & Simon Housego, 852-863. Proceedings Ascilite Sydney 2010. http://ascilite.org.au/conferences/sydney10/procs/Sankey-full.pdf.

Scheiter, Katharina. & Peter Gerjets. 2007 Learner control in hypermedia environment. *Educational Psychology Review* 19: 285-307.

Starr-Glass, David. 2018. Building Learning Spaces: Creating Online Learning Environments. In *Online Course Management: Concepts, Methodologies, Tools and Applications* edited by Information Resources Management Association's, 241-257. USA: IGI Global.

In: The Impact of COVID-19 on Teaching ...   ISBN: 978-1-53619-947-5
Editors: S. Studente, S. Ellis et al.   © 2021 Nova Science Publishers, Inc.

Chapter 5

THE EFFECT OF MITIGATION STRATEGIES ON UNIVERSITY STUDENT'S MENTAL HEALTH AND WELL BEING: A REVIEW OF PRELIMINARY STUDIES

Sylvie Studente*, PhD
Stephen Ellis, PhD and Bhavini Desai, PhD
Regent's University London, London, United Kingdom

ABSTRACT

Rising levels of anxiety, stress and depression have been recognised as common psychological responses to the pandemic (Rajkumar, 2020). The number of people experiencing anxiety disorder in the UK has doubled during the pandemic (Kwong et al., 2020), with similar trends reported worldwide (Xiong, et al., 2020). In response to the pandemic, universities closed their physical premises, suspended face-to-face teaching, and moved to online modes of delivery. Implementing online learning has been necessary to enable students to continue with their studies. However, research reports that the effects of the migration to online learning has impacted student's social and psychological wellbeing (Zhai & Du, 2020;

* Corresponding Author's E-mail: sylvie.studente@regents.ac.uk.

Prowse et al., 2020). This chapter provides a review on preliminary studies undertaken in the area on student's mental health and wellbeing during the pandemic, and concludes with recommendations to assist in supporting students during this challenging time.

Keywords: mental health, wellbeing, socialisation, higher education

1. INTRODUCTION

The impact on psychological health as a consequence of the COVID-19 pandemic has been widely reported (Torales et al., 2020). Specifically, lockdown restrictions have led to increased levels of anxiety, stress, and depression (Wang et al., 2020; Marques et al., 2021; Brooks et al., 2020). These markers are recognised as common psychological responses to the pandemic (Rajkumar, 2020). In the United Kingdom alone, the number of people experiencing anxiety disorder has doubled during the pandemic (Kwong et al., 2020). These findings are not exclusive to the United Kingdom, similar trends have been reported in Germany (i.e., Bäuerle et al, 2020), France (i.e., Husky et al, 2020), Bangladesh (i.e., Islam et al, 2020), China (i.e., HeWang et al, 2020), Poland (i.e., Wang et al., 2020), and Spain (i.e., Ozamiz-Etxebarria et al, 2020) amongst other countries worldwide (Xiong, et al., 2020).

In response to the pandemic, universities closed their physical premises, suspended face-to-face teaching, and moved abruptly to online modes of delivery. Despite the physical closure of campuses, universities have generally responded well in providing innovative teaching and learning online to continue providing education to students despite restrictions (Sandhu & de Wolf, 2020). Implementing online learning was necessary for students to continue with their studies. However, research reports that the effects of the migration to online learning has impacted student's social and psychological wellbeing (Zhai & Du, 2020; Prowse et al., 2020). Preliminary studies undertaken into the mental wellbeing of students during the pandemic report that although some students have responded to changes in educational strategies with resilience (Kelley, 2020), many have reported detrimental impacts to their mental health (Nania et al, 2020). It is likely that the closure of university campuses has led to feelings of uncertainty and anxiety for some students (Padron et al., 2021). This chapter provides a review of preliminary studies undertaken in the area on student's mental health and wellbeing during the pandemic, and concludes with recommendations to assist with supporting students during this unprecedented time. However, it should not be forgotten that a key purpose of a university education is to increase the independence of thought and action for individual students and as such the degree of scaffolding erected to support students has to be proportionate to enabling students to become independent learners in their own right.

2. BACKGROUND MOTIVATION

2.1. Impacts on Mental Health Wellbeing

Under usual circumstances, students seem to be generally concerned with their academic performance (Mikolajczyk, 2008). In the case of first year students, the transition from school to university would place this group under stress ordinarily, as they are placed in a new environment and need to learn to study more independently than at school (Parker et al., 2004). In the case of international students, this group ordinarily face stress related to acculturation in studying abroad (Smith & Khawaja, 2020). The closure of university campuses, the move to online delivery, along with reduced opportunities for social interaction have further exacerbated stressors overall for students (Grubic et al, 2020; Medha et al, 2020; Odriozola-González et al, 2020; Sahu, 2020). Owing to the increase in "stressors," students have been faced with pressures to learn independently, many students have reported a decline in motivation towards their studies, and drop-out rates have increased as a consequence of the move to online learning and lack of opportunities for social integration. Current research reports worldwide trends in increased stress levels, anxiety, and depression amongst university students (Liu, 2020; Rajab & Alkattan, 2020). Although some scholars have reported no significant mental health changes during the pandemic (i.e., Fried, 2020), the general consensus in the area of research is that the physical restrictions have been detrimental to students psychological wellbeing in a number of ways.

Academic performance is often judged by students in comparison to peers. In normal settings this can be done informally by seeing how peers are reacting and contributing to the learning process. Students can see if others in the group are 'getting it' when debates or questions occur. Judgements relating to effort and time spent learning can also be made through comparisons and informal support from other students. In the online delivery world these opportunities are significantly diminished. Education through zoom calls is a very isolating model whereby it is very difficult to maintain interactions, and to judge how other students are responding, especially when the model does not require web cameras to be switched on. This issue should be interpreted as a two-way problem, as the lecturer is often also unable to effectively 'gauge the room' by sensing whether the learning they were anticipating is working as planned, or whether they need to change tack. An experienced lecturer will be able to respond to their student's needs and frustrations by amending the lesson structure on the fly, over a zoom call this is less likely to happen as the flexibility is inevitably restricted.

The transition to remote learning alongside other anxieties is reported to have impacted the mental wellbeing of students (Laher et al., 2021), especially for those who have little prior experience in online learning (Piotrowski & King, 2020), and also, those experiencing problems with reliable internet access, availability of webcams and/or computers (Bolatov et al., 2020). Overall increases in levels of anxiety and depression experienced by students have a number of detrimental impacts in terms of academic performance and progression (Mudenda et al, 2020), struggling to focus on academic studies (Kecojevic et al., 2020), and decreased engagement and motivation with studies (Duraku & Hoxha, 2020). Although the closure of university campuses and the implementation of online learning have been necessary, these strategies have also caused disruption to student learning and social interaction with peers and lecturers. The following section discusses social impacts on students.

2.2. Changes in Social Dimensions

In times of crisis, social support is essential for people's wellbeing. However, owing to lockdown measures, students report feeling socially isolated from their peers and lecturers (Boda et al, 2020). First year students in particular may feel that they have missed out on the experience of being able to form bonds, and establish new friendships with classmates. In addition, reduced social interaction has negatively impacted students who live alone (Bolatov et al., 2020; Kawachi et al, 2001). Reductions in social interaction, feelings of loneliness and a lack of social support are associated with declining mental health (Wang et al., 2020).

Critical social dimensions for student's wellbeing include interaction, friendship, social support, and co-studying. The limitations imposed on these social dimensions are reported to be associated with detrimental impacts on mental health, such as depression, anxiety, stress, and loneliness (Elmer et al., 2020; Tambag et al, 2018). Social isolation in itself can lead to elevated anxiety and symptoms of depression (Hortulanus, 2006; Chaturvedi et al., 2021). This has also had an impact on student's academic performance because when students are socially engaged with peers, they are more likely to be motivated with their studies (Furrer & Skinner, 2003). Some students will be strongly motivated by a desire to compete and to be seen as achieving. The lack of social interaction inevitably restricts such perceptions. The dimensions of social wellbeing and mental health are of critical importance to student's overall wellbeing, motivation, performance, progression with their studies and overall engagement. The following section provides a review of preliminary studies on student's social and mental wellbeing during the pandemic.

3. A REVIEW OF PRELIMINARY STUDIES

A study conducted by Cao et al., (2020) reported that 25% of students reported an increase in anxiety and other psychological impacts correlated with the imposing of lockdown measures. A survey conducted by Young Minds (2020) also reports that 83% of students surveyed stated that the effects of the pandemic has further escalated pre-existing mental health conditions due to the physical closure of campuses, restrictions on socialisation, and loss of daily routine. Similar findings have been reported by Wang et al., (2020) who surveyed 2031 undergraduate and graduate students. Results from the study indicated that 48% of students reported moderate to severe levels of depression, 38% reported moderate to severe levels of anxiety and 71% reported that stress and anxiety levels had increased as a result of the physical closure of the university. Similar findings were reported in a study conducted by Fu et al., (2021), in which 89,588 students were surveyed. Findings reported that 41% of students experienced anxiety.

Elmer et al. (2020) conducted a study investigating COVID-19 related stressors among 212 undergraduate students. Findings from the study reported that student's levels of anxiety, stress, depression and loneliness were exacerbated as a result of the pandemic. Additionally, physical isolation and lack of socialisation were associated with detriments to overall mental health. Other studies have focused upon emotions, behaviours, and overall wellness, such as that conducted by Copeland et al., (2021). In the study, 675 first year university students completed an assessment at the beginning of the 2020 term, and then again during the onset of the COVID-19 pandemic. Results from the study reported that students had experienced a persistent impact on mood, emotions, and wellness as a consequence of educational mitigation strategies due to the pandemic.

A study conducted at a UK university by Evans et al., (2021) surveyed 254 undergraduates. Findings reported a significant rise in symptoms of depression. These reported trends are not specific to the UK, a number of worldwide studies have also stated similar findings. In a study conducted by Faisal et al., (2021) 874 students in Bangladesh were surveyed. Findings from the study state that 72% of students reported symptoms of depression, and that 40.2% reported symptoms of anxiety. Similar findings arise from a study conducted by Fruehwirth et al., (2021) in which 419 first year undergraduate students at an American university participated. Again, students completed a survey, the results from which indicate that 25.3% of students reported feelings of anxiety, and 31.7% reported symptoms of depression. An examination of the findings concluded feelings of increased anxiety and depression were correlated with social isolation and distance learning (as opposed to face-to-face). A study from Poland conducted by Debowska et al., (2021) reports upon data collected from 7,228 university students during the first two months of the pandemic. Again, the results indicated a significant increase in reported depression levels as the pandemic progressed.

3.1. International Students

Preliminary studies have also focussed upon the impact on international students who have had to return to their home countries and continue their studies online. An example comes from a study conducted by Lai et al., (2020) who surveyed 124 International students, who had returned home once lockdown measures were first announced. Findings indicate that 84.7% of students reported moderate to high stress levels, and 12.1% of students reported symptoms of depression. Negative wellbeing was reported to be associated with the change to remote teaching and learning, uncertainties regarding studies, and a lack of social support.

4. DISCUSSION AND CONCLUSION

Lockdown restrictions have led to reported increases in levels of anxiety, stress, and depression amongst university students as common psychological responses to mitigation measures. Despite restrictions, universities worldwide altered their delivery and continued to provide education to students online. Although such mitigation strategies have been a necessity, there have been both social and psychological consequences for students. Preliminary studies reviewed within this chapter indicate that while some students have responded to changes in the provision of education with resilience, many have reported detrimental mental health issues associated with increased levels of anxiety, loneliness, and depression. These issues have been reported worldwide as a consequence of the physical closure of campuses, restrictions on socialisation, feelings of isolation, loss of daily routine, low mood, lack of social support, uncertainties regarding studies, and the change to distance learning, which have arisen as a consequence of mitigation strategies. Students ordinarily feel pressure in terms of their academic performance, and in the case of first year students, common stressors are learning to study more independently in a new environment. In the case of international students, common stressors include acculturation in studying abroad. For students choosing to complete their education in an international environment the pandemic has been a bitter blow. Not only have they had all of the privations that non-international students have, but their desire to experience their learning in a different country has been severely restricted. It could be argued that these students have had the worst deal, as the non-academic elements of the university experience that are the most difficult to translate into an online world, such as socialising, networking, interesting societies, sporting, and cultural events cannot be lifted and shifted into cyberspace well. In some ways the very essence of what the student was hoping to achieve, by exposure to culture and life in a new surrounding has all but been denied. Whether this leads to a reassessment of the value of international education options, or is a temporary blip remains to be seen.

The response to the pandemic has exacerbated stressors overall for students. The shift to online education has posed additional stressors to certain groups of students, particularly, for those who have little prior experience of distance education, also, some students may have faced additional barriers in accessing online educational resources due to issues of reliability of internet connection, and the availability of hardware. Impacts upon student's mental wellbeing during the pandemic has resulted in some instances in a decline in motivation towards studies, increasing drop-out rates, students struggling to focus on learning materials, a decline in academic performance and progression. It has required a swift and unexpected shift to a very different learning style, which for some might be a tough step compared with the more supportive environment they were accustomed to and expecting. Online education requires a high degree of consistent self-motivation, with far less of the 'extra' benefits of a peer group around as support. We have seen how the progress of Massive Open Online Courses (MOOCS) has been beset by very low completion rates as the flush of enthusiasm for learning withers for some over time, and the reality of isolated studying kicks in.

Preliminary studies have also highlighted that social support is essential for mental wellbeing, and that mitigation strategies deployed by universities during the pandemic have not only disrupted student learning and mental wellbeing, but also affected social interaction with peers and lecturers. While first year students in particular have not had the opportunity to establish necessary friendships with classmates, students in general have reported feeling socially isolated from their peers. These reductions in social interaction, although necessary, have adversely affected the mental wellbeing of students. Currently, research purports that declines in student's mental wellbeing will likely continue for as long as the pandemic continues, and its effects may even continue to recur for longer.

The preliminary studies reviewed within this chapter highlight the urgent need for strategies to support student's metal health and wellbeing. In light of this, a number of recommendations are made.

- Reduce the disruption to learning as far as possible by providing certainty where possible in terms of programme details, likely return dates etc.
- Assist students with developing coping mechanisms through the development of 'learning to learn' strategies.
- Provision of mental health and support services.
- Outreach to students who require extra support in their studies.

- Establish new and effective methods of social contact and interaction amongst students such; as chatbots, action learning sets, virtual check ins etc.
- Provide opportunities for students to connect with their peers.
- Host social events online, giving students opportunities to connect with their peers and lecturers in informal settings. Extend the touchpoints for students to be able to reach out to their lecturers as and when they feel anxious regarding their studies.
- Implement online programmes to promote the mental wellbeing of students.

It is important that interaction and socialisation for students is facilitated, and the use of online social technology could be an effective solution for this, (which has already been previously discussed within this edited book). The concerns emphasised within this chapter are that the dimensions of social wellbeing and mental health are of critical importance to student's overall wellbeing, motivation, performance, progression with studies, and overall engagement. This chapter has presented a review of preliminary research within the area, and provided recommendations to assist in supporting student's mental health and well-being in this unprecedented and uncertain time.

We do have to guard carefully against any new measures that are developed and expanded to deal with the current crisis becoming the norm for the future. A university experience is about exploration, risk taking, and challenging oneself to be the best you can. If we surround every student with an all-pervasive protection package, rather than a reasonable support scaffold, they will not be enabled to develop and mature into independent, confident, and reflective learners. Going to university is a key step in the life of many and can be truly life changing. But becoming life changing is not achieved by always staying in the safe, comfort zone of past-experience, it comes from self-realisation and achieving one's own goals.

Students both current and potential are increasingly accustomed to living a 'curated life'. That is, they are supported much more in terms of what to do, how to think, and what to experience. The online world is becoming increasingly effective in targeting experiences (to individuals based on their known profile, or past history). Perhaps the university sector has a real opportunity to catch up in this regard. Wouldn't it be amazing if every student, arriving for the first at a new place of study, was greeted with a welcome that did not just signpost all the myriad of support and resources they could avail themselves of, but rather an individualised package of 'curated guidance' tailored just for them that would highlight the most relevant aspects of their new university life? Technology and learning analytics data allow us to learn more about individual students. In addition, many students expecting that they will be increasingly treated as individuals, not simply a number in a large 'factory based' programme. These two factors can hopefully come together beneficially to allow students to get the most out of their university experience and drive scarce university resources to the places where they will be most impactful.

REFERENCES

Bauerle, A., Teufel, M. & Musche, V. (2020). Increased generalized anxiety, depression and distress during the COVID-19 pandemic: a cross-sectional study in Germany. *Journal of Public Health.* doi: 10.1093/pubmed/fdaa106.

Boda, Z., Elmer T., Vörös, A., & Stadtfeld, C. (2020). Short-term and long-term effects of a social network intervention on friendships among university students. *Scientific Reports.* 10, 1. Pp 1 – 12.

Bolatov, A., Seisembekov, T., Askarova, A., Baikanova, R., Smailova, D. & Fabbto, E. (2020). Online-learning due to COVID-19 improved mental health among medical students. *Medical Science Educator.* 31. Pp 183 – 192.

Brooks, S., Webster, R., Smith, L., Woodland, S., Wessely, N., Greenberg, G. & Rubin, J. (2020). The psychological impact of quarantine and how to reduce it: rapid review of the evidence. *Lancet,* 395. Pp. 912 – 920.

Cao, W., Fang, Z., Hou, G., Han, M., Xu, X., Dong, J., & Zheng, J. (2020). The psychological impact of the COVID-19 epidemic on college students in China. *Psychiatry Research*. 287, Article 11298.

Chaturvedi, K., Vishwakarma, D. & Sing, N. (2020). COVID-19 and its impact on education, social life and mental health of students: a survey. *Children and Youth Services Review*. Vol 121. 105866.

Copeland, W., McGinnis, E., Bai, Y., Adams, Z., Nardone, H., Devadan, V., Rettew, J. & Hudziak, J. (2021). Impact of COVID-19 pandemic on college student mental health and wellness. *Journal of the American Academic of Child & Adolescent Psychiatry*. 60, 1. Pp 134 – 141.

Debowska, A., Horeczy, B., Boduszek, D. & Dolinski, D. (2020). A repeated cross-sectional survey assessing university students' stress, depression, anxiety, and suicidality in the early stages of the COVID-19 pandemic in Poland. *Psychological Medicine*. 1 – 4. doi: 10.1017/ S003329172000392X.

Duraku, H. & Hoxha, L. (2020). *The impact of COVID-19 on higher education: a study of interaction among student's mental health attitudes towards online learning, study skills and changes in student's life*. Retrieved from https://www.researchgate.net/publication/ 341 599684.

Elmer T., Mepham K., Stadtfeld C. (2020). Students under lockdown: Comparisons of students' social networks and mental health before and during the COVID-19 crisis in Switzerland. *PLoS ONE*. 15(7).

Evans, S., Alkan, E., Bhangoo, J., Tenenbaum, H. & Knight, T. (2021). Effects of the COVID-19 lockdown on mental health, wellbeing, sleep, and alcohol use in a UK student sample. *Psychiatry Research*. 298. 113819.

Faisal, R., Jobe, M., Ahmed, O. & Sharker, T. (2021). Mental health status, anxiety and depression levels of Bangladeshi university students during COVID-19 pandemic. *International Journal of Mental Health & Addiction*. doi: https://doi.org/10.1007/s11469-020-00458-y.

Fried, E. (2020). Mental Health and Social Contact During the COVID-19 Pandemic: *An Ecological Momentary Assessment Study*. Retrieved from https://doi.org/10.31234/osf.io/36xkp.

Fruehwirth, J., Biswas, S., & Perreira, K. (2021). The COVID-19 pandemic and mental health of first-year college students: Examining the effect of COVID-19 stressors using longitudinal data. *PLoS ONE.* 16, 3. e0247999.

Fu, W., Yan, S., Zong, Q., Anderson-Luxford, D., Song, X., Lv, Z. & Lv, C. (2021). Mental health of college students during the COVID-19 epidemic in China. *Journal of Affective Disorders. February* 2021. Pp 7 – 10.

Furrer, C. & Skinner, E. (2003). Sense of relatedness as a factor in children's academic engagement and performance. *Journal of Educational Psychology.* 95, 1. Pp 148 – 163.

Grubic, N., Badovinac, S. & Johri, A. (2020). Student mental health in the midst of the COVID-19 pandemic: a call for further research and immediate solutions. *International Journal of Social Psychiatry.* doi: https://doi.org/10.1177/0020764020925108.

HeWang, Z., Yang, H., Yang, Y., Liu, D., Li, Z., Zhang, X., Zhang, Y., Shen, D., Chen, P., Song, W., Wang, X., Wu, X., Mao, C. (2020). Prevalence of anxiety and depression symptoms, and the demands for psychological knowledge and interventions in college students during COVID-19 epidemic: A large cross-sectional study. *Journal of Affective Disorders.* 275. Pp 188 – 193.

Hortulanus, R., Machielse, A., Meeuwesen, L. (2006). *Social Isolation in Modern Society.* London; Routledge.

Husky, M., Kovess-Masfety, V. & Swendsen, J. (2020). Stress and anxiety among university students in France during COVID-19 mandatory confinement. *Comprehensive Psychiatry*, 102. p. 152191.

Islam, M., Barna, S., Raihan, H., Khan, M., & Hossain, M. (2020). Depression and anxiety among university students during the COVID-19 pandemic in Bangladesh: a web-based cross-sectional survey. *PLoS One,* 15. Pp. e0238162.

Kawachi I., & Berkman L. (2001). Social ties and mental health. *Journal of Urban Health.* 78, 3. Pp 458 – 46.

Kecojevic, A., Basch, C., Sullivan, M. & Davi, N. (2020). The impact of the COVID-19 epidemic on mental health of undergraduate students in New

Jersey, cross sectional study. *Plos One.* September 2020. doi: https://doi.org/10.1371/journal.pone.0239696.

Kelley, S. (2020). *Students face pandemic disruption with resilience.* Retrieved from https://news.cornell.edu/stories/2020/04/students-face-pandemic-disruption-resilience.

Kwong, A., Pearson, R., Adams, M. & Northstone, K. (2020). Mental health during the COVID-19 pandemic in two longitudinal UK population cohorts. *Psychiatry and Clinical Psychology.* June. doi: 10.1101/2020.06.16.20133116.

Laher, S., Bain, K. & Bemath, N. (2021). Undergraduate psychology student experiences during COVID-19: challenges encountered and lessons learnt. *South African Journal of Pscyhology.* March. doi:10.1177/0081246321995095.

Lai, A., Lee, L., Wang, M., Feng, Y., Lai, T., Ho, L., Lam, S., Ip, M. & Lam, T. (2020). Mental Health Impacts of the COVID-19 Pandemic on international university students, related stressors, and coping strategies. *Frontiers in Psychiatry.* November. doi: 10.3389/fpsyt. 2020.584240.

Liu, C., Pinder-Amaker, S., Hahm, H. & Chen, J. (2020). Priorities for addressing the impact of the COVID-19 pandemic on college student mental health. *Journal of American College Health.* doi:https://doi.org/10.1080/07448481.2020.1803882.

Mudenda, S., Zulu, A., Phiri, M., Ngazimbi, M., Mufwambi, W., Kasanga, M. & Banda, M. (2020). Impact of Coronavirus disease (COVID-19) on college and university students: a global health and education problem. *Aquademia.* 4, 2 Article No: ep20026.

Marques, G., Drissi, N., Torre Diez, I., Abajo, B. & Ouhbi, S. (2021). Impact of COVID-19 on the psychological health of university students in Spain and their attitudes towards mobile mental health solutions. *International Journal of Medical Informatics.* 147.

Meda, N., Pardini, S., Slongo, I., Bodini, L., Zordan, M., Rigobello, P., Visloi, F. & Novara, C. (2021). Student's mental health problems before, during and after COVID-19 lockdown in Italy. *Journal of Psychiatric Research.* 134. Pp 69 – 77.

Mikolajczyk, R., Maxwell, A., El Ansari, W., Naydenova, V., Stock, C., & Ilieva, S. (2008). Prevalence of depressive symptoms in university students from Germany, Denmark, Poland, and Bulgaria. *Social Psychiatry and Psychiatric Epidemiology.* 43, 2. Pp 105 – 112.

Nania, T., Dellafiore, F. & Caruso, R. (2020). Risk and protective factors for psychological distress among Italian university students during the COVID-19 pandemic: The beneficial role of health engagement. *International Journal of Social Psychiatry.* July 2020. doi: https://doi.org/10.1177/0020764020945729.

Odriozola-González P., Planchuelo-Gómez Á., Irurtia M., & de Luis-García R. (2020). Psychological effects of the COVID-19 outbreak and lockdown among students and workers of a Spanish university. *Psychiatry Research.* 290.

Ozamiz-Etxebarria, N., Dosil-Santamaria, M., Picaza-Gorrochategui, M. & Idoiaga-Mondragon, N. (2020). Niveles de estrés, ansiedad y depresión en la primera fase del brote del COVID-19 en una muestra recogida en el norte de España Cad. *Saúde Pública,* 36, 4. Pp e00054020. [Levels of stress, anxiety and depression in the first phase of the COVID-19 outbreak in a sample collected in the north of Spain Cad. *Public Health*]

Padron, I., Fraga, I., Vieitez, L., Montes, C. & Romero, E. (2021). A study on the psychological wound of COVID-19 in university students. *Frontiers in Psychology.* January. https://doi.org/10.3389/fpsyg.2021.589927

Parker, J., Creque, R., Barnhart, D., Harris, J., Majeski, S., Wood, L., Bond, B., & Hogan, M. (2004). Academic achievement in high school: Does emotional intelligence matter? *Personality and Individual Differences,* 37. Pp 1321 – 1330.

Piotrowski, C. & King, C. (2020). COVID-19 pandemic: challenges and implications for higher education. *Education.* Vol. 141. Pp 61 – 66.

Prowse, R., Sherratt, F., Abizaid, A., Gabrys, R., Hellemans, K, Patterson, Z. & McQaid, R. (2020) Coping with the COVID-19 pandemic: examining gender differences in stress and mental health among university students. *Frontiers in Psychology.* doi: https://doi.org/10.3389/ fpsyt.2021.650759.

Rajab, M. & Alkattan, K. (2020). Challenges to online medication education during the COVID-19 pandemic. *Cureus.* 12, 7.

Rajkumar, R (2020). COVID-19 and mental health: a review of the existing literature. *Asian Journal of Psychiatry.* 52. p. 102066.

Sahu, P. (2020). Closure of universities due to Coronavirus disease 2019 (COVID-19): impact on education and mental health of students and academic staff. *Cureus.* 12:e7541. 10.7759/cureus.7541.

Sandhu, P. & de Wolf, L. (2020). The impact of COVID-19 on the undergraduate medical curriculum. *Medical Education Online.* 25, 1.

Smith, R. & Khawaja, N. (2011). A review of the acculturation experiences of international students. *Int. J. Intercult. Relat.* (2011) 35:699–713. 10.1016/j.ijintrel.2011.08.004.

Tambag, H., Turan, Z., Tolun, S., & Can, R. (2018). Perceived social support and depression levels of women in the postpartum period in Hatay. *Nigerian Journal of Clinical Practice.*

Torales, J., Higgins, M., Castaldelli-Maia, J., & Ventriglio, A. (2020). The outbreak of COVID-19 coronavirus and its impact on global mental health. *International Journal of Social Psychiatry.* doi:https://doi.org/ 10.1177/0020764020915212.

Wang, Z., Yang, H., Yang, Y., Liu, D., Li, Z., Zhang, X., Zhang, Y., Shen, D., Chen, P., & Song, W. (2020). Prevalence of anxiety and depression symptom, and the demands for psychological knowledge and interventions in college students during COVID-19 epidemic: A large cross-sectional study. *Journal of Affective Disorders.* 275. Pp 188 – 193.

Xiong, J., Lipsitz, O., Nasri, F., Lui, L., Gill, H., Phan, L., Chen-Li, D., Lacobucci, M., Ho, R., Majeed, A. & McIntyre, R. (2020). Impact of COVID-19 pandemic on mental health in the general population: a systematic review. *Journal of Affective Disorders.* 277. Pp 55 – 64.

Young Minds. (2020). *Coronavirus: Impact on young people with mental health needs.* [online]. Available from: https://youngminds.org.uk/ media/3708/coronavirus-report_march2020.pdf.

Zhai, Y. & Du, X. (2020). Addressing collegiate mental health amid COVID-19 pandemic. *Psychiatry Research.* 288. doi: 10.1016/ j.psychres. 2020.113003.

In: The Impact of COVID-19 on Teaching ...   ISBN: 978-1-53619-947-5
Editors: S. Studente, S. Ellis et al.   © 2021 Nova Science Publishers, Inc.

Chapter 6

WELLBEING IN THE TIME OF COVID

Stephen McKenzie, PhD, Michelle I. Jongenelis, PhD and Litza Kiropoulos, PhD*

School of Psychological Sciences, University of Melbourne,
Melbourne, Australia

ABSTRACT

The COVID-19 pandemic has had serious and as yet not fully understood effects on our world, including our education systems. There have been substantial effects of COVID that are relatively temporary and also effects that may well turn out to be much more lasting. Whilst COVID is not the cause of the recent proliferation of online courses and course components in primary, secondary, and tertiary education, it is an accelerator of efforts to increase online learning offerings. It is important to recognise the valuable contemporary truth in the old adage that every cloud has a silver lining. This principle can valuably be applied to creating opportunities for transforming great education system problems into great education system solutions. The University of Melbourne is Australia's highest internationally ranked university and deeply values both the non-academic and academic success of its staff, students, and broader community in which it operates. The University responded to the COVID

* Corresponding Author's E-mail: stephen.mckenzie@unimelb.edu.au.

crisis by developing and offering online wellbeing-enhancing resources for staff, students, and health professionals to assist people respond optimally to their COVID-related wellbeing challenges. These challenges included staff and students' sudden isolation and full immersion in online education and also health professionals suddenly having to manage their own and their clients' isolation and other psychological and physical health challenges.

This chapter describes The University of Melbourne's development and implementation of three innovative and potentially transferable online education COVID responses: 1. A student wellbeing and success orientation module, 2. A series of free short online courses for health professionals, and 3. A series of free short online courses for students. These offerings successfully met temporary and ongoing needs for large scale wellbeing-, success-, and health-enhancing online education resources.

Keywords: COVID-19, online education, wellbeing

INTRODUCTION

The University of Melbourne has over 50,000 students and almost 9,000 academic and professional staff, and is Australia's highest internationally ranked university.

The University and its largest faculty – Medicine, Dentistry and Health Sciences (FMDHS) – was faced with substantial challenges caused by the COVID-19 induced lockdown of the University in 2020, which led to the sudden replacement of its traditional physical education capacities with online capacities.

The University responded to the emerging known and unknown effects of this crisis by recognising the unmet psychological, social, emotional, and physical wellbeing needs of students, as well as recognising their academic success needs and the inter-relationship of these needs. The sudden transition of online learning and teaching from a rising learning and teaching modality to a risen modality provided great educational challenges that needed to be met with significant educational and also related physical and psychological wellbeing improving solutions.

To meet its accelerated and far-reaching online education and related needs, the University and its health faculty developed and implemented new and far-reaching online courses and course components including:

- A Student Life orientation subject – Your wellbeing and success – which will be offered to all new students of the University from 2022.
- A series of free online short courses for health care professionals, produced by the University's Mobile Learning Unit for health-related online program production.
- A series of free online short courses for all staff and students, produced by the University's MSPACE general online program production unit.

This chapter describes each of these innovative online education programs that were developed in response to both COVID induced and also ongoing whole student education challenges, and provides examples of the development and implementation of each of these special online programs.

The chapter also includes a concluding section on the overall impact and significance of these potentially transferable responses to common COVID-related and other ongoing educational challenges.

'YOUR WELLBEING AND SUCCESS' ONLINE MODULE, IN THE 'JOINING MELBOURNE' STUDENT ORIENTATION SUBJECT

The University of Melbourne's response to the COVID crisis included the development of wellbeing- and success-related online material for all of its new students via the inclusion of a *Your Wellbeing and Success* module in a new *Joining Melbourne* online orientation subject. A list of all of the modules in the subject is provided in Figure 1.

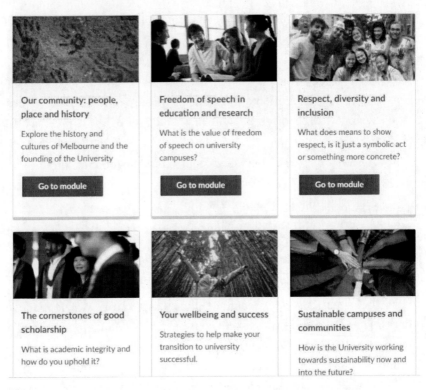

Figure 1. Starting page for the six *Joining Melbourne* orientation subject modules.

The *Your Wellbeing and Success* module was conceived by and developed for the University by its School of Psychological Sciences, and will be given to all of the University's new students from 2022. The module will help the University's new students be optimally ready for University student life by assisting them to:

- Feel fully connected to other students and to the University, via online as well as non-online resources.
- Feel part of and fully engaged in the greater University and University student community, via online as well as non-online contacts (Adam 2020; Dolan et al. 2017).
- Successfully transition from secondary school learning and life to University learning and life.

Content

The online *Your Wellbeing and Success* module in the *Joining Melbourne* subject will provide a dynamic, student-centred, appealing and challenging learning environment for large numbers of new students. The module will educate students by helping them achieve optimal understanding and experiences of wellbeing and success, as well as providing them with wellbeing- and success-supporting and enhancing information and resources. The education aspect of the module includes a challenging of students to go beyond their usual ideas about wellbeing and success, to consider what these concepts really are, and what they really mean to them.

The content and structure of the module will encourage new students to consider wellbeing and success as inter-related systems with psychological, physical, and social components, and to consider whether success at university just means academic success, or whether it also includes whole person success, including wellbeing, connection, and personal growth.

The module was developed within and will be offered within the Canvas Learning Management System, and it includes innovative online education features that enable online course offerings to be much more than repositories of recorded live lectures and readings. This advancement of early online education capacities is analogous to what the new television medium eventually achieved after starting out as a not-fully-new medium that merely provided 'radio with pictures' (McKenzie, Garivaldis and Dyer 2020).

The *Your Wellbeing and Success* orientation module, and also the other innovative online offerings described in this chapter, is built around the development of an e-Workbook – an electronic study guide – that provides a guiding narrative for and links to the module's diverse and engaging multimedia learning materials.

These purpose-built online learning materials include interactive learning activities and videos, as well as static information and resources. High levels of expert technical support were provided by the University and its health faculty – including from expert learning designers and video producers – to support the academic content experts' development of the special online programs.

The *Your Wellbeing and Success* module within the *Joining Melbourne* student orientation subject is designed to:

- Challenge, expand, and deepen students' usual way of thinking about wellbeing and success, and to encourage them to recognize that whole student success includes wellbeing and connection success (Chung and McKenzie 2020).
- Provide education, information, and resources from a student's eye view to help engage students and provide them with learning materials and processes that are fully relevant to them (Verenikina et al. 2017).
- Connect students with University student life supporting academic and non-academic resources, by creating new resources and introducing and linking students to existing resources.
- Provide a dynamic, student-centred learning experience that helps students be active contributors to and co-designers of their optimal wellbeing and success at the University.

Features

Workbook

A guiding narrative that includes links to videos, learning activities, and other resources, structured into:

1. Introduction to the module.
2. Wellbeing-related education, principles, information, and resources.
3. Success-related education, principles, information, and resources.

Resources

Including information about and links to existing University resources, such as those offered by its Counselling services, library and academic services, and clubs and societies. The skill developing resources featured in the module include learning activities, information, and ongoing practices to support:

- Study skills
- Connection
- Mindfulness
- Resilience
- Behaviour change

Videos

Four videos were created for and used in the course:

1. An introduction to the module from its creators.
2. Student wellbeing questions asked by students and answered by a wellbeing expert.
3. Tips for achieving academic and non-academic student success provided by ongoing students of the University.
4. Tips for positively changing behaviours presented by students of the University.

The opening page and video of the module is shown in Figure 2.

Interactive Learning Activities

These consist of:

1. A starting reflection and discussion on what success means to each student.
2. A reflection on what transitions each student is experiencing.
3. Building a success plan.
4. A reflection on what wellbeing really means to each student.
5. Trying a mindfulness practice.
6. Adaptive and maladaptive coping strategies.
7. Deep communication activity (assessed).

An example of a learning activity is shown in Figure 3.

1.0 Overview of 'Your wellbeing and success' module

Welcome to the 'Your wellbeing and success' module. This module will help your student experience to be successful and enjoyable by giving you actual student challenges, solutions, resources, information and practices that will help you achieve your best possible study, wellbeing and life success. The module will help you make the transition into university life in the best way possible, including by bringing success and wellbeing to life – to your life.

Watch - Welcome to the module

Discover more about the module and what it offers you.

Figure 2. The opening page of the *Your Wellbeing and Success* module, including its first video.

[Wellbeing] 2.0 Discussion: What is student success? A⁺
Venica Evans
All Sections

Of course you want to be successful at university, but how do you define success as a student? Success can mean different things to different people. In this activity you will consider what being successful means to you personally.

Time: 15 minutes (for reflection and response)

Task (10 mins)

Consider:

1. What does success mean to you?
2. What does success at university mean to you? Is it achieving high marks or is it more than that to you?
3. Is your definition different from your family or friends? Explain.

Share your thoughts by posting below.

Length

Approximately 50 words, or 2-3 sentences.

Peer feedback (5 mins)

Once you have made your post you will be able to see other's replies, check out other posts by your fellow students.

Read and respond to two other peers' posts.

- When responding to others it is good to address the person by naming them (for example, "Hi Than").
- You may also want to acknowledge something they've said by complimenting (for example, "You made a great point about ...") or support/agree with something they mentioned (for example, "I had a similar experience ..." or "Like you, I ...")

Source: Peer feedback strategies from Verenikina, I., Jones, P. T. & Delahunty, J. (2017). *The Guide to Fostering Asynchronous Online Discussion in Higher Education.* Available from: www.fold.org.au/docs/TheGuide_Final.pdf.

Figure 3. Defining student success activity and discussion.

Course Outcomes and Impact

The courSe [course] has been completed and is ready to be offered to all new students of the University from 2022. As part of the co-design of and student involvement in the completed module, a draft version of it was given to a group of students who provided comments and suggested refinements. The completed module had high levels of student satisfaction and met its objectives of (i) fully engaging and challenging students via the use of a student perspective, (ii) giving students a valuable wellbeing and success education, and (iii) providing students with useful information, skills, and resources.

Course Reflections

The development of this module was a great opportunity to use innovative online education features, capacities, and principles to introduce new students to the University and the challenges and opportunities of tertiary education, including those related to COVID. The course provided valuable challenges to its developers as well as to its eventual recipients. These included the challenge of constantly providing information and experiences from a student's perspective and helping students discover their own learnings and learning pathways.

FREE SHORT ONLINE COURSES FOR HEALTH PROFESSIONALS

The University of Melbourne's Faculty of Medicine, Dentistry and Health Sciences responded to the COVID crisis by calling for the development of short, free online courses that help a wide range of health professionals optimally respond to the sudden emergence and proliferation of COVID-related physical and psychological health challenges.

The following principles were used to underpin the development and offering of these courses:

- Perceived need for evidence-based and sound information on relevant issues for health care professionals.
- Part of the Faculty's commitment to educating health care professionals.
- Part of the suite of responses by the Faculty in providing information and education about COVID and its impact.

The courses were:

- Developed and offered online to enable health care professionals in any location to access them easily.
- Offered free for reasons of equity and access.
- Produced and offered quickly through the Faculty's Mobile Learning Unit.
- Successful, with high enrolments (over 10,000 total course enrolments to date), and of great benefit to the many health professionals who have completed them.
- High quality, with a sound pedagogical approach.

The following tables provide details of the courses.

Table 1. COVID-19 MDHS free short online courses descriptions

Date of Release	Department	Project description
March 2020	Population Health	Communicating COVID-19
April 2020	Surgery	COVID Lung Ultrasound
April 2020	Nursing	Critical Care Essentials for Nurses
April 2020	Population Health	COVID-19 Ethics
April 2020	Medical Education	Clinician Resilience during COVID-19
April 2020	School of Psychological Sciences	Compassion Fatigue: The cost of caring
Oct 2020	Surgery	COVID-19 Lung and Cardiac Ultrasound

Table 2. COVID-19 MDHS free short online courses names and enrolment number as of March 2021

☐ Course Name: Clinical Ethics and COVID-19 (1,189 records)
☐ Course Name: Clinician Resilience during COVID-19 (1,253 records)
☐ Course Name: Communicating COVID-19 (2,893 records)
☐ Course Name: Compassion Fatigue: The Cost of Caring (1,265 records)
☐ Course Name: Critical Care Essentials for Nurses (2,645 records)
☐ Course Name: UEG - COVID-19 Lung and Cardiac Ultrasound (1,221 records)
Grand Totals (10,466 records)

The following chapter section provides a description of one of these courses as an example.

Compassion Fatigue: The Cost of Caring in Health Professionals

Compassion Fatigue: The cost of caring in health professionals is an online short course that explores compassion fatigue, vicarious trauma and burnout, who is at risk of developing compassion fatigue, signs and symptoms of compassion fatigue, contributing factors, understanding warning signs and triggers, and practical strategies for managing compassion fatigue.

Who is This Course For?

The course was designed for anyone working in caring and health professional roles, especially those in high stress, trauma-exposed environments such as healthcare and frontline emergency staff (i.e., staff working in emergency departments, ICU, acute hospital wards, mental health).

Introduction

Professionals in the fields of health care and emergency first responders (e.g., nurses, emergency and ICU staff, medical staff working with specific populations such as oncology, general practitioners and mental health care) are at a higher risk for compassion fatigue (CF) and vicarious trauma (VT) than the general population. When professionals are overloaded, are working with a lot of traumatic content, have a heavy caseload with clients who are chronically in crisis they can experience a higher than normal level of compassion fatigue. The course showed health professionals how to recognise and respond to the physical, emotional, cognitive and behavioural signs of compassion fatigue.

Physical Signs of Compassion Fatigue

- Physical exhaustion and fatigue
- Sleep disturbance – difficulty sleeping or settling at the end of the day or wanting to sleep too much
- Reduced interest in sex due to feeling depleted
- Headaches, migraines, digestive issues, nausea, aches, tension and pain that are related to emotional stress

Emotional/Cognitive Signs of Compassion Fatigue

- Emotional exhaustion, reduced ability to feel empathy
- Low patience
- More easily angry, irritable, cynical and resentful
- Shifts in your ability to relate with compassion to clients or loved ones
- Hypervigilent (being 'on guard'), feeling anxious, panicky, increase in irrational fears

- Problems in personal relationships outside of work due to reduced compassion
- Doubting your competence and skill as a helper/clinician
- Feeling helpless towards clients
- Depressed mood (feeling hopeless about yourself, clients and the future)
- Suicidal thinking
- Diminished sense of satisfaction or enjoyment in your career
- Insensitivity to emotionally charged material
- Poor concentration or focus, memory difficulties
- Dread of working with certain clients/patients
- Flashbacks and intrusive thoughts
- Intrusive imagery or dissociation
- Disruption to world view

Behavioural Signs of Compassion Fatigue

- Distancing or isolating yourself from others
- Not engaging in activities you typically enjoy
- Low motivation
- Difficulty making simple decisions or clinical decisions that affect clients/patients
- Absenteeism - missing work, taking sick days
- Dreading or avoiding clients/patients
- Frequently changing jobs or leaving the field of work
- Compromised care towards certain clients (disconnecting)
- Disordered eating
- Increased use of alcohol or drugs to cope
- Difficulty separating work and personal life (impaired boundaries)
- Being the caretaker in your personal life

- Problems with intimacy and personal relationships
- Difficulty separating work life from personal life

What Can Be Done to Prevent Compassion Fatigue?

The course showed health professionals how to address compassion fatigue by developing self-care strategies and an understanding of early warning signs of compassion fatigue. Self-care is what people do for themselves to establish and maintain health, and to prevent and deal with illness.

The following is a list of self-care strategies that were provided in the course to assist health professionals in preventing and managing compassion fatigue.

1. Take stock of your commitments and determine whether you can change any of these
2. Develop a self-care idea list.
3. Find time for yourself every day. Undertake one enjoyable and nourishing activity every day.
4. Delegate work. Ask for help at home and at work.
5. Have transition time or an activity between work and home.
6. Learn to say no.
7. Create a 'trauma filter' to protect yourself from high levels of trauma input.
8. Learn to recognize the signs and symptoms of your own compassion fatigue and learn effective strategies to manage these.
9. Join a peer supervision/ support group.
10. Attend professional training in the area of compassion fatigue.
11. Consider cutting back your hours and exposure to trauma.
12. Exercise.

Course Outcomes and Impact

So far over 1200 health professionals have successfully completed the compassion fatigue free short online course.

FREE SHORT ONLINE COURSES FOR STUDENTS

The University of Melbourne's FMDHS responded to the COVID-19 health, social, and education crisis by calling for the development of short, free online courses that successfully met a temporary yet ongoing need for large scale wellbeing enhancing online resources, information, and education for staff and students across the University.

The *Wellbeing in the Time of COVID* short course series consisted of three related courses for students across the University – *Mindfulness Techniques for Improving Wellbeing, Resilience Techniques for Improving Wellbeing*, and *Behaviour Change Techniques for Improving Wellbeing*. The following chapter section provides a description of one of these courses as an example.

Behaviour Change Techniques for Improving Wellbeing

The COVID-19 pandemic has had an unprecedented impact on everyday life. Human behaviour has been forced to change instantaneously, with people in every country experiencing restrictions of varying degrees of severity.

While these sacrifices were in aid of the noble cause of protecting public health, their impact on wellbeing cannot be overestimated. Habitual patterns of behaviour, such as going to work or the gym and socialising with others, were thrown into disarray.

The Behaviour Change Techniques for Improving Wellbeing [course] was developed to help staff and students of the University develop behaviours that will help them deal with the pandemic.

Figures 4 and 5 provide examples of course content.

Image by Alexas Fotos from Pexels

Change only takes place through action… – The Dalai Lama

Action may not always bring happiness; but there is no happiness without action – Benjamin Disraeli

Taking action to change our behaviour involves a number of internal or psychological processes. Many of these processes are within our control. What do you think these might be? Write your response below.

Figure 4. The Behaviour change techniques for improving wellbeing short course's opening page.

Course Aims

Minimising the impact on wellbeing of this sudden change to our lives was deemed critical. The third and final course in the *Wellbeing in the time of COVID* series – *Behaviour Change Techniques for Improving Wellbeing* – featured 8 modules, each of which provided participants with information on the concrete steps they can take to improve their physical and psychological health. Led by three behavioural scientists, the course aimed to:

1. Provide participants with a theoretical and practical understanding of behaviour change;
2. Motivate participants to take action to change their behaviour to improve their wellbeing; and
3. Assist participants develop and effectively work toward achieving their health and wellbeing goals.

Course Content

It was important to ground the course in behaviour change theory to ensure participants were knowledgeable of the underlying evidence-base for the techniques being taught.

To that end, the course began with a brief overview of the core concepts of behaviour change.

Participants were presented with a model detailing the following concepts:

- Motivation – desire to engage in a behaviour
- Self-efficacy – believing you can succeed with something
- Goal setting – setting a defined goal that will guide future behaviour
- Self-monitoring – examining and recording what you do
- Feedback – reviewing how well you have done in meeting a set goal
- Evaluation – assessing the extent to which you have succeeded in reaching a set goal
- Goal review – reconsidering a goal in light of feedback and evaluation

Subsequent modules provided more detailed yet easily digestible information on these concepts and, crucially, presented concrete strategies in which participants could engage to increase the success of their behaviour change journey. Specifically, these subsequent modules focused on:

1. Motivation and self-efficacy
2. SMART goals
3. If-then planning
4. Self-monitoring, self-evaluation, and goal review
5. Habit formation

While the course was developed to assist its learners to improve their wellbeing during COVID-19, the information presented did not focus solely on behaviour change during the pandemic. The techniques featured in the course offer benefits beyond pandemic times.

4.0 Introducing SMART goals ♪

Image by Markus Winkler from Unsplash

Setting goals is the first step in turning the invisible into the visible - Tony Robbins

People with goals succeed because they know where they're going - Earl Nightingale

In Module 3, you learnt about how to motivate yourself to take action to improve your wellbeing. In this module, we harness this motivation to develop SMART goals, which are essential to our efforts to change our behaviour.

Not all goals are created equal. 'I will work on my fitness' is very different to 'I will go to the gym three times this week and exercise for one hour on each of those occasions'. The first goal is vague and ambiguous – when will you work on your fitness? What does 'working on' your fitness mean? The second goal is

Figure 5. A course content example - smart goals.

Learning Mechanisms

Course content was primarily delivered via a series of lecture-style videos between 10-20 minutes in duration. These videos were complemented by recommended readings, YouTube videos, and external websites.

To increase engagement with the course and assist them in their behaviour change journey, participants were encouraged to complete a series of activities as part of an eJournal. This initially involved selecting a behaviour from their own life they could change to improve their wellbeing (e.g., reducing alcohol intake, quitting smoking, becoming more physically active, eating healthily, improving sleep habits, spending more quality time with family and friends, reducing procrastination, etc.). The content being delivered in each module was then used to enhance this activity. For example:

At the conclusion of the module on motivation and self-efficacy, participants were encouraged to note their motivation for changing the behaviour they chose and assess confidence in their ability to change that behaviour. Specifically, they were asked to:

- List the costs of their current behaviour and the benefits of change.
- Note why they wanted to change their behaviour and whether their desire to change was strong enough to challenge their existing desires.
- Note the ways in which they could weaken their current desires, how they could replace any losses, and whether there were any substitutes or alternatives to their behaviour.
- List the positives of taking action and link these positives to their values.

At the conclusion of the module on SMART goals, participants were encouraged to set a SMART goal that required them to do something more than once over the subsequent week in relation to the behaviour they wanted to change. They were also asked to note how they would record their progress toward this goal. At the conclusion of the module on if-then planning, participants were encouraged to think about the behaviour they wanted to change and for which they developed a SMART goal and developed one to two 'if-then' plans that will help them achieve this goal. At the conclusion of the module on self-monitoring and self-evaluation, participants were asked to note whether they had been monitoring their progress regularly and well and, if not, what tools they could use to better monitor their progress. They were also asked to reflect on:

- What had helped them change their behaviour.
- What obstacles they have faced and whether there were any if-then plans they could specify to overcome these obstacles.
- How they were feeling as they attempted to change their behaviour.

- Whether they were rewarding themselves for good progress.
- Whether they were being kind to themselves for slow progress and taking steps to improve.
- Whether they needed to review and/or adjust their goal.

At the conclusion of the module on habit formation, participants were asked to note any habits they had that they would like to break and reflect on:

- The cues in their environment that trigger this habit.
- What they can do to avoid these cues.
- What they can do to disengage when they encounter a cue.
- Any alternative behaviour in which they can engage instead.

Course Outcomes and Impact

This and the other two short courses in the series have been and are still being offered at no cost to all staff and students of the University. To date over 400 staff and students have successfully completed *Mindfulness Techniques for Improving Wellbeing*, over 200 have successfully completed *Resilience Techniques for Improving Wellbeing*, and over 100 have successfully completed *Behaviour Change Techniques for Improving Wellbeing*.

Course Reflections

The development of the course, while rewarding, was challenging. The behavioural scientists involved in delivering the content were each experiencing varying degrees of COVID-19 restrictions. It was hoped that restrictions would be relaxed, allowing the video content to be developed on campus with state-of-the art recording facilities. When it became apparent that this was not to be, we had to use the techniques being taught in the course to adjust to the times and change our own behaviour. Videos were recorded in our homes, where constant battles were fought with the birds and motorcyles that interjected our teaching. Video content for each module was recorded at least 3 to 4 times before we decided to change our own behaviour and perfectionist tendencies and accept that a bird chirping in the background was not such a big deal after all.

CONCLUSION

COVID-19 has had substantial effects on tertiary education that are relatively obvious, and has also had insidious and potentially more damaging effects, the significance of which may not be fully apparent for some time. The potentially damaging effects of COVID to academic and also non-academic aspects of education need to be fully addressed, creatively and courageously. The total COVID-related education challenges that need to be addressed include challenges to students' sense of belonging to, and being fully connected and engaged with, their whole tertiary learning environment.

Achieving equivalence of online education with traditional education is less straightforward for education intangibles such as sense of community and engagement than it is for academic aspects of education. These broader aspects of total educational equivalence that need to be achieved in and after the time of COVID will help optimise online education; allowing it to give students a full online education that includes emotional and physical wellbeing and job and life readiness. The time has come for online education to reveal silver linings to the COVID clouds by providing creative and courageous responses to our great education challenges. We have a great opportunity to direct COVID-related and ongoing online education challenges to the noble goal of achieving total online educational equivalence with non-online education, including in students' sense of educational community, engagement, wellbeing, and job and life readiness.

The special online programs that were developed by The University of Melbourne in response to the educational and broader challenges of COVID-19 included online course content that extends the capacity of health professionals, staff, ongoing students, and new students to respond optimally to new and accelerated education and health challenges, including to physical and psychological wellbeing. The University of Melbourne's health and wellbeing improving free short courses and orientation module are providing a wide range of valuable COVID response skills and resources to a wide range of health professionals, staff, and students that will help them to not only survive in but also thrive in our beyond COVID world.

REFERENCES

Adam, Emily. (2020). "No student is an Island – Online Students Perspective of Sense of Community in Online Education". In Stephen McKenzie, Filia Garivaldis and Kyle R. Dyer (Eds.), *Tertiary Online Teaching and Learning: TOTAL Perspectives and Resources for Digital Education*. Springer, Singapore.

Chung, Jen., McKenzie, Stephen. (2020). "Is it Time to Create a Hierarchy of Online Student Needs?" In Stephen McKenzie, Filia Garivaldis, and Kyle R. Dyer (Eds), *Tertiary Online Teaching and Learning: TOTAL Perspectives and Resources for Digital Education*. Springer, Singapore.

Dolan, Joanne, Kain, Kevin, Reilly, Janet and Bansal, Gaurav. (2017). "How Do You Build Community and Foster Engagement in Online Courses?" *New Directions for Teaching and Learning*, (151), 45 - 60.

McKenzie, Stephen, Garivaldis, Filia, Dyer, Kyle. (2020). "Preface". In Stephen McKenzie, Filia Garivaldis and Kyle R. Dyer (Eds), *Tertiary Online Teaching and Learning: TOTAL Perspectives and Resources for Digital Education*. Springer, Singapore.

Verenikina, Irina, Jones, Pauline and Delahunty, Janine. (2017). *The Guide to Fostering Asynchronous Online Discussion in Higher Education*. Available from: www.fold.org.au/docs/TheGuide_Final.pdf.

In: The Impact of COVID-19 on Teaching ...   ISBN: 978-1-53619-947-5
Editors: S. Studente, S. Ellis et al.   © 2021 Nova Science Publishers, Inc.

Chapter 7

EXAMINATION OF THE FUTURE FOR LECTURES AND SEMINARS FOR STUDENTS - IN BUSINESS MODULES, IN THE 21ST CENTURY

*Philip Mayer**

Lecturer, Oxford Business College, Oxford, United Kingdom

ABSTRACT

This chapter will explore the value and usefulness of lectures and seminars in delivering information to learners today and in the future. Teaching and lecturing are concerned with many facets. However, the two key aspects of the learning experience for any student are the content of the courses and how they are delivered. These two intertwined topics are the subject of this chapter. Most teachers are very comfortable delivering lectures and seminars with materials given to them by others, however often they need to adapt, modify, change or indeed construct their own courses too. Therefore, the course delivery and design are vital to the success and development of educators. Indeed, Jones talked about the "triadic" relationship of teaching being made up of three elements: the

---

* Corresponding Author's E-mail: Phillip.mayer@oxfordbusinesscollege.ac.uk.

teacher, the learner and the material (Jones, 2005, p. 5). This chapter will look at delivery and design of the material, i.e., lecturing and course design, from the teachers' and learners' perspectives. What lectures are and how they are delivered will be examined with some relevant theories and examples will be given from the writer's professional experience.

INTRODUCTION

This writer's own definition of the term lecture is:the passing on of information from one to many in a suitable space for a specified time. The lecturer is the one, the audience, usually students or learners, is the many. A simple definition of the word lecture gives, something similar, but with an emphasis on the educational lecture:

"An educational talk to an audience, especially one of students in a university" (Oxford Dictionaries, 2015).

Another definition helps to put this chapter into context:

"The term 'lecture' is teacher centred: it says what teachers do. The important thing is what are students doing while the teacher is lecturing." (Biggs & Tang, 2011).

So, with **Biggs'** definition in mind, this chapter will explore what teachers do when they teach. However, students should be kept at the forefront of the analysis throughout this chapter. Indeed, in commercial terms, a business (or college) will have its greatest successes where they are focused on satisfying its customers' (or students') demands. Likewise, the best universities and colleges should endeavour to focus on satisfying itsstudents' educational experience. The chapter will consider this question: how relevant are lectures in higher education today? This chapter will include an examination and exploration of some theories around both lecturing and course design, as well as looking at some practical applications of these theories taken from some examples of the writer's experiences as a teacher, lecturer and executive trainer.

THE VALUE OF THE LECTURE

Steve Jones (2007) reiterates the longevity and effectiveness of lectures was being questioned by Dr Samuel Johnson as far back as 1766.

"Talking of education, 'People have now a-days ... got a strange opinion that everything should be taught by lectures. Now, I cannot see that lectures can do so much good as reading the books from which the lectures are taken... 'Lectures were once useful; but now, when all can read, and books are so numerous, lectures are unnecessary. If your attention fails, and you miss a part of a lecture, it is lost; you cannot go back as you do upon a book!" Johnson (cited in Osgood, 1917, pp. 62, 195).

So if, Dr Johnson was questioning the relevance of the lecture nearly 250 years ago, with the onset of the new medium of books, it is not surprising that the new technologies of today, offer a similar or even greater challenge. One more recent development came from The Open University. The Open University was started in the UK in 1969, by Geoffrey Crowther. This suggested a new challenge to more traditional teaching, by offering distance learning via television, radio and post. Crowther stated that they had the intention of reaching those that had been unable to access traditional higher education, i.e., "the tired, the poor, the huddled masses" (Konnikova, 2014). Then, even more recently, there has been further challenges from the prevalence of online courses, which most educators have seen as a support and expansion of more conventional teaching (Garrison, 2004).

Online teaching embraced another concept in 2011 when MOOCs (Massive Open Online Courses), started to become seen as the next big development in lecturing. The original thinking was that these courses would be able to reach a new learner audience. Professor Sebastian Thur, a star lecturer from Stanford, was able to reach 160,000 students with one lecture, within three months of his online broadcast on artificial intelligence, with little or no cost to these students. This was being hailed as an amazing advancement in access to higher education. Indeed, The New York Times talked about, "The Year of the MOOC" (Pappanonov, 2012).

In November 2014, there were 495 MOOCs (five times as many as in 2013), listed on the MOOC aggregator (Class Central, 2014, Konnikova, 2014). Although, enrolment has soared completion rates have been very low, between 5% and 13% (Perna, 2013). The most successful students, attending MOOCs, were those already well educated, self-motivated and generally in least need of MOOCs. This ran counter, to the original goals of those that started their MOOCs platforms, who harked back to Crowther's stated aims for the Open University, i.e., education for those who had been denied access previously, through circumstances and lack of resources (Howland, 2002). MOOCs have had a mixed success, thus far, some studies have shown that people are using MOOCs as a new online resource, with a similar commitment as that of a mobile app (Koller, 2013). MOOC providers could improve their delivery with use of "Control Theory." This was developed by Patrick Suppes and Richard Atkinson in 1962, they developed this for very young children, of varying abilities, doing online learning. They developed systems that allowed students to work at different rates, i.e., brighter students worked faster and longer without interruptions, while less able students were given assessments and stopping points, more frequently. If this principle were applied to MOOCs the more impersonal approach of 'one size fits all' could be tailored to students (Konnikova, 2014).

Therefore, the impersonal touch, of online courses in general and MOOCs in particular suggests that the demise of the traditional lecture is still premature. Perhaps it will be modified to embrace the new technologies, further. This writer regularly encourages his students to embrace online resources and often plays suitable short video clips, during seminars, to stimulate discussion. The students could visit these clips themselves and often they do, after the lecture. However, the impact of seeing them together and then having a meaningful discussion as a group is powerful and thought provoking. This author also likes to use humorous cartoons – however, the teacher must know their audience. Recently, one seminar student, questioned the cartoons used by another lecturer – explaining he was not a fan of British humour.

TEACHING STYLES AND THEORIES

Behaviourism

This can be considered old school, traditional teaching; whereby students, are persuaded down a path using various techniques, rewards and encouragement. Behaviourism looks at conditioned responses. Students are seen as coming with a blank page, whereby they can be taught by instruction, given ideas and work on the principle that they will respond to stimuli. This leads to a more teacher centred approach (Ertmer, 1993).

Behaviourism dates back to the late 1800's. When Pavlov did his work, he found that dogs started to salivate with the promise of food. Pavlov was a scientist and was originally just measuring salivation in dogs as a scientific experiment. However, during his research, he found that these dogs not only reacted to receiving their food, but also some of the triggers, before they even received their meals. Pavlov found that when he, or his technicians, entered the lab or even just rang a bell (before actually giving the dogs their food), this triggered the same salivation reaction as the giving of the food itself. Also, he found that he was able to reverse these responses by operating the triggers, e.g., ringing the bell and not giving the food, over time the salivation stopped (Mcleod, 2007). This underlies the theory of behaviourism. Humans actually react to certain words and expressions, expecting certain conditions to follow. When people talk in encouraging soothing tones, this elicits compliance and vice versa, i.e., harsh tones and expressions encourage non – compliant behaviours and responses. This is the foundation of old school, traditional teaching and teacher led education. The traditional risk and reward, teaching seemed to be based on this premise. Students respond to good marks and encouragement positively; they also sometimes have fear of failure (Duit, R & Treagust, D. F. 1998).

Many students plead with their teachers to tell them the answers to the questions and theories that are being explored. Some teachers (including this author), will encourage them to find their own answers through discussion and self-research, which could be said to be a more constructivist approach (see below). The concept, that behaviourism is the simple idea that students are merely empty vessels; waiting for their teachers to fill them with knowledge, theories and ideas has been questioned by several academics, including Fox 2001, Meyer 2009 and Hager 2009. It can be said that theories and models are usually simplifications and generalisations based on analysis of numerous real situations. Therefore, acceptance of theories should be taken for guidance purposes only and academics should make their own judgements based on their own experiences, research and evidence.

Constructivism

"Viewpoint in learning theory which holds that individuals acquire knowledge by building (on) it from innate capabilities interacting with the environment" (Schulte, P. L., 1996).

This definition of constructivism is where educators look to build on the knowledge and understanding that learners already have absorbed from their environment. Students and learners arrive at their course with some prior knowledge and experience, even if not directly relevant. Then the learner builds or constructs further knowledge and understanding on top of the prior knowledge. This is more student centred, focusing on what the students need to do, diametrically opposed to behaviourism, where teachers lead students. There is also a sense of self development and self- building. Biggs talks about constructivism originating from cognitive psychology and he traces it back as far as Piaget (1950), (Biggs & Tang, 2011). Also, further learning is obtained by the learning in the same learning styles, methods 'schemata' that learners are used to. Biggs said that these theories only formalised how more enlightened teachers already taught (Biggs & Tang, 2011 p. 22).

In commercial terms, a company listens to its customers, a successful company gives customers what they want and demand. Likewise, a successful teacher will listen to his/her learners and teach them in a style and format that they can understand. It is to be recommended (in the opinion of this writer), to strip the concepts and principles down to basics and use practical examples.

For example, when talking about teamwork, in a recent class, a video was shown of the Jamaican 4 x 100m relay team, at the London 2012 Olympics. This was a wonderful example of effective teamwork, at its best. Usain Bolt could not have won that gold medal and broken that world record on his own, i.e., he needed the support and excellence of his teammates. This example demonstrates to learners, the power and vital need to support each other in their studying and learning environment. All can benefit from the support, guidance and interaction with others on courses and in team working too (Husbands C. 2013).

Biggs favours the constructivist approach, students come with various levels of knowledge and experience and they can build on this, construct more knowledge. Constructivism gives more power back to the students. This makes for a more student centred approach (Biggs & Tang, 2011).

Some argue that constructivism is merely the way good teachers teach anyway. There are several academics that question the validity and importance of constructivism (Fox, 2001, Meyer, 2009, Hager, 2009).

People really learn best by doing things, many teachers believe in making their classes and courses, as practical as possible. Indeed, the workshops that this writer delivered to civil service staff were designed to embed the learning learnt pre - course. This demonstrated that the success of putting ideas into action, through group activities, does reinforce the learning experience. People remember far less, when they read, of course this can vary according to levels of interest and how engaged readers are too. Some people, including this writer, are more interested to read about areas of business, than areas of natural science. Thus, it is best to always consider the context of such assertions (Johnston, P. H., & Winograd, P. N. 1985). Also, Johnston (1985) suggests that as learners progress from a more passive approach to a more active approach to learning, they will remember, learn and absorb more and more. In other words, learners learn by doing. Lectures that engage learners in activities, discussions, enquiries and investigations, are far more interesting and effective (Biggs, 2011).

High Quality of Lecture Delivery

Dr Michael Motley suggests that people have either a performance or a communications orientation (Motley, 1997). The first of these concepts is more concerned with how speakers perform.

Performance Orientation

Many teachers come from the viewpoint that it matters how they perform their teaching. The origin of this, according to Motley (1997), usually comes from a childhood experience of delivering a talk to classmates, e.g., reciting a poem or a famous piece of writing. The delivery of this talk would be judged by the classmates and the teacher predominantly on the delivery, how well did they stand, talk and deliver. This experience tends to stay with most people until later on in life and when adults are delivering a speech, talk, seminar and/or lecture most people, with this perspective, will be worried about their performance, tone of voice, body language and being judged by the audience/students (Motley, 1997). This, says Motley, and this writer concurs, in the main, leads to less effective communication. The other type of orientation is more concerned with the effectiveness of communication.

Communication Orientation

When speakers simply worry about the message or the communication reaching the audience that are their recipients, rather than being concerned with their performance per se, they can be much more effective communicators. Motley gives an example of a fellow student who froze and actually broke down in tears, as she was delivering her prepared speech to her college classmates, which included Michael Motley. She was so worried about giving a perfect performance. However, the professor did not let her sit down (when she lost her thread in her memorised talk), which seemed harsh at first, instead he started to ask her questions about her prepared talk and she answered him haltingly at first, but then she gained more confidence. In the end by answering his questions and focusing on speaking to him – rather than the class, she finished her talk and this experience enabled her to become one of the best presenters of her college (Motley, 1997, p. 51). The author of this chapter had a similar epiphany when he attended a self – development course, many years ago (Landmark Education, 2015); during this course they did a 'fear' exercise whereby people realised there was no need to fear the judgement of others, since others are not really judging them, they are thinking about themselves and that others are judging them too. This experience helped this writer's perception to shift away from (worrying about his) performance and move towards a more communication centred orientation. Of course, it is natural to still be concerned about the performance aspects, but usually it is possible to be genuinely more interested in delivering the message to others. This has enabled, this writer, to be a much more effective communicator and now he really enjoys communicating to his learners, regardless of the size or location of the group. He believes this is a really crucial factor for the importance, success and relevance of the lecture. If lecturers can communicate their messages effectively, then students will be interested to attend to hear these messages. He likes to ask his students questions to recap, e.g., what was discussed last week, before the break etc. Also, it is a good idea to get students to engage in activities prior to and during class (Mazur, 1998).

The Dr. Fox Effect

Michael Fox, an experienced professional actor (with film credits), was hired to lecture to a group of senior medical academics in 1970 by three researchers, John E. Ware, Donald H. Naftulin and Frank A. Donnelly, in the USA. This experiment proved a great success, although the content, of the lecture, was nonsense, the excellent delivery by Fox (as the fake Dr Myron Fox) 'bamboozled' the expert audience (Schneider, 2008). Most teachers, even those, such as this writer, with good knowledge of business and business concepts, commercial experience and several years of training, will still have great concerns about their depth of knowledge and complete understanding of every aspect of business topics. However, they can take some comfort in the Dr Fox Effect, proving a triumph of delivery over substance is possible. However, although this idea can be comforting, it is advisable to take great caution over using this as a principle to teach, as there is still an overall requirement for teachers to have depth of knowledge, understanding of concepts and solid substance (Kavale, K. A, 1987). It is recommended that teachers continue to use their vast experience and knowledge gained during their careers, with further input from ongoing research, self-development and self-study.

FURTHER CONSIDERATIONS

It is important to think about what students want to get out the lecturing experience. For example, when teaching adult learners, who are coming back to studying after a break from education and also maybe with better knowledge of old-style teaching – a more behaviourist approach. They frequently make requests of their teachers to tell them all the information. However, they should be reminded that the teacher is only one resource, for their learning, they have other resources, i.e., lecture slides, books, Moodle or Blackboard, or other VLEs (virtual learning environments), journals, web sources and each other. Eric Mazur (1998), a physics lecturer at Harvard, took this concept even further, setting questions, via email, to his students asking them what they found interesting or challenging prior to the lecture. If there were no answers, then there would be no admittance to the lecture. In this way he was able to tailor his lecture to his students' interests and/or concerns. He also got students to answer multiple choice questions in the lecture. His intention was to make his lectures more interactive and more student-focused. He was regularly voted teacher of the year (Biggs, 2011, p. 139). Also, David Yamane (2006), a sociology lecturer, looked at course preparation assignments (CPA), whereby he asked his students to look at writing an assignment on a particular question or idea prior to class, then discussing this in class. Some teachers give feedback to students in class, where the teacher discusses their assignments with them, individually, and how they could improve these (Biggs, 2011, p. 140). Also, teachers can summarise some general points for feedback to discuss with the whole class.

However, if teachers are able to incorporate more of Mazur and Yamane's approaches to make their classes even more relevant and interesting to their students. This can move teaching away from the more traditional stand and teaching approach, which is less effective (Biggs 2011, p. 137). However, the idea of, "making the lecture theatre a learning theatre," (Biggs, 2011, p. 139), is very appealing and ultimately necessary for the ongoing success of most students. This point reinforces the message i.e.that more activity and more engagement leads to better learning outcomes. Now to link these concepts and to consider.

Alignment

Many educators, including this writer, find it challenging to deliver material to large groups, including, adult learners, whether in college or executive training courses. The connection of the material, the learners and the teachers, is the alignment that Biggs and Tang so keenly addressed (Biggs, 2011). So,if teachers consider themselves strong communicators, is that enough? They should be careful not to fall into the trap of being convinced of the success of the Dr Fox Effect when teachers sometimes worry that they do not have enough knowledge about their subjects. However, if they can encourage students to be more proactive in their learning, see the learning as a joint effort, a more constructivist approach, they can support the students to their successful development. This next section will consider some curriculum theory to form a link between delivery and content.

CURRICULUM

Many teachers are very comfortable delivering lectures, seminars, workshops and generally teaching, coaching or training people whether they are students, delegates on a course or business people in groups or one to one. However, some are not as comfortable when it comes to designing courses and curriculum. This is why course design is so important. Definition of Curriculum:

> "A programme of activities (by teachers and pupils) designed so that pupils will attain so far as possible certain educational and other schooling ends or objectives" (Grundy, 1987).

Grundy said that the curriculum is mindful of what the students and teachers do and focused on the outcomes of the students. How to get there is an interesting journey. To start this journey, consider the curriculum in terms of four types of gardens (Ross, 2000). Subjects can be seen as the equivalent of the arrangement of plants and foliage in four different types of gardens, i.e., baroque, natural, utilitarian and cottage. This concept portrays a very powerful image (Hughes et al., 2015). Considering teaching and learning as the growing and development of minds given the appropriate nurturing environment. The concept was first introduced by the then Minister of Education in 1959: "David Eccles, minister of education, 1959 – shifted focus to what was actually being taught" – 'open up the secret garden of the curriculum' (Ross, 2000).

The Secret Garden(s) of the Curriculum: Baroque Garden

This is like the following curriculum - very rigid, old style, traditional, clearly defined structured, walled garden no overlapping, lack of linkage between subjects/topics, idealistic, - curriculum of clearly distinct subjects, each has its own tradition and form of cultivation. This is the course that is very much teacher led, i.e., content, pace, style all coming from the teacher. Examples could be individual old school subjects – rigid stand -alone subjects, e.g., latin, sciences, mathematics – i.e., factual based subjects with little room for debate (Ross, 2000). Some examples include some of the curriculum materials imposed on this author, e.g., certain undergraduate syllabus teaching and the Capita course material for civil service seminars, could come into this category of rigid stand-alone courses. However, fortunately he had the freedom to move around this rigidity. The teaching in this category is more traditional, in style, less interactive and more orientated to stand and deliver style.

Natural Garden

This is like the following curriculum – loose boundaries between what may or may not be admitted. The subjects, topics, knowledge and ideas are taken from every day, real life situations. This is far more learner focused. However – the looseness and lack of focus and direction can be misleading for the learners, lead to confusion and give mixed messages. Examples could be artistic courses, design and self - taught subjects, i.e., the students go on a tour of self-discovery (Ross, 2000). Most teachers should encourage their students to do their own digging around the subjects. Therefore, although this might be seen as an unlikely analogy for business courses and seminars – there are definitely aspects of the natural garden approach. This writer talks about his personal/professional real life business experiences and uses case studies extensively too; and he also encourages the learners to bring their own experiences and examples too. This helps to explain and clarify concepts to the learners.

"Dig for Victory"

This is like the following curriculum - useful and practical learning which prepares students for their future roles in the workplace. There is a strong connection between education and skills for work or vocation. This equates to the behaviourist approach. Examples could be apprenticeships, specific vocational training – even courses for the professions, with specific instructions, e.g., accountancy, law and medicine, i.e., learning in a step by step way (Ross, 2000). Many teachers and executive trainers equate their practical experiences and applications in their courses. For example, in the civil service training courses (the writer used to deliver these) - the staff are sent by their departments to enhance their 'on the job' skills. Also, when teaching business modules to adult learners and undergraduates, they are regularly encouraged to see how the topics that are being investigated can be applied to their work and business situations. For example, looking at topics such as leadership and motivation in organisational behaviour or human resource management - students are encouraged to look to see how these can that be applied to their company/job/staff, now or in the future.

Cottage Garden

This is like the following curriculum - the courses have developed this way over a number of years – grown naturally, but in an organised way. Examples of these could be modules or courses that have developed and evolved over the years, being altered by their teachers/lecturers in a progressive way. Many courses are repeated each year with minor modifications. For example, human resource management and business & management of small medium enterprises, these courses are repeated and modified each year (Ross, 2000).

CONCLUSION

Lectures and seminars remain important and relevant for learners on business courses. Most teachers enjoy delivering material to groups, whether this is their own material or content given to them. Inevitably many teachers are still using some aspects of behaviourist, spoon fed, old style, teaching; but the modern approach is that most teachers are consciously trying to be more constructivist in their approach. In other words, teachers try to encourage their students to build on their existing knowledge and experiences, during seminars and/or courses. Further, some teachers are concerned about their content knowledge and effective communication. However, it is comforting to take some optimism engendered by the evidence of the Dr Fox effect, whereby teachers can be even more confident that style is as important, but not more so, than substance (Schneider, 2008).

Also, teachers should remember that having a communication orientation continues to stand them, in good stead, for getting their clear messages across to their learners (Motley, 1997).

If lectures and seminars have lasted over 250 years beyond Dr Johnstone's forecast of doom, it seems safe to forecast that future generations will still be experiencing these in their education (Jones, 2007). However, no doubt future business courses might look somewhat different to those of today. There will probably be much more use of technology, online resources and self-study. So long as educators remain sensitive to students' demand for both design and delivery of material – the MOOCs and the future variations of MOOCs, can be used to enhance the use of face-to-face interaction. It is worth acknowledging that there has been a dramatic increase of the use of online teaching and training (especially in the last twelve months), and with the increased use of social media; however, people still want to meet others, in person, to truly interact. Likewise, with education, future business students will still want to interact with other students and teachers, in the forum of the lecture and seminar, both online and face to face.

The prevalence and proliferation of online teaching, especially in the last twelve months, has hastened the used of modern technology for seminars and lectures. However, the future of lectures and seminars in business modules looks mainly optimistic, strong and positive. There will be continual changes and development in course delivery and design. However, as long as teachers, learners and the materials can remain in alignment, there will be continuity in the construction of a strong educational future for all.

REFERENCES

Biggs, J. B., Tang, C. (2011). *Teaching for quality learning at university: what the student does.* (4th Ed.). Maidenhead: McGraw-Hill: Society for Research into Higher Education and Open University Press.

Class Central. https://www.class-central.com/ (Accessed 10.04.20).

Duit, R., and Treagust, D. F. (1998). 1.1 *Learning in Science-From Behaviourism Towards Social Constructivism and Beyond.*

Ertmer, P. A. and Newby, T. J. (1993). Behaviourism, Cognitivism, Constructivism: Comparing Critical Features from an Instructional Design Perspective. *Perf. Improvement Qrtly*, 6: 50-72. doi: https://10.1111/j.1937-8327.1993tb00605.

Fontbin, P. (2015). *Senior Lecturer at Regent's University London.*

Fox, R. (2001). 'Constructivism Examined,' *Oxford Review of Education*, 27(1), 23-35.

Garrison, D. R., and Kanuka, H. (2004). Blended learning: Uncovering its transformative potential in higher education. *The internet and higher education*, 7(2), 95-105.

Guerriero, M. (2014). 'A MOOC Mystery: Where Do Online Students Go?' *The New Yorker,* 28th February, p. available at: http://www.newyorker.com/news/news-desk/a-mooc-mystery-where-do-online-students-go (Accessed: 10.04.20).

Hager, P. and Hodkinson, P. (2009). 'Moving beyond the metaphor of transfer of learning,' *British Educational Research Journal*, 35(4), 619-638.

Howland, J. L. and Moore, J. L. (2002). 'Student Perceptions as Distance Learners in Internet-Based Distance Education,' *Distance Education,* 23(2), pp. [Online]. Available at: http://www.tandfonline.com/doi/abs/10.1080/0158791022000009196#.VSfpoqFwbbg (Accessed: 10.04.20).

Hughes, et al., (2015). Clare Bentall, Andrea Creech, Gwyneth Hughes and Holly Smith. *Designing Courses and Curricula* - Seminar January 2015.

Husbands, C. (2013). *Sprinting: Training, Techniques and Improving Performance*. Crowood.

Johnston, P. H., and Winograd, P. N. (1985). Passive failure in reading. *Journal of Literacy Research*, 17(4), 279-301.

Jones, E. S. (2007). Reflections of the Lecture: outmoded medium or instrument of inspiration? *Journal of Further and Higher Education* 31. (4), p. 397-406 doi: https://10.1080/0309877070165816.

Jones, G. (2005). *Gatekeepers, Midwives and Fellow Travellers: Learning Alignments and Pedagogy in Adult Education*: Mary Ward Centre.

Kavale, K. A. and Forness, S. R. (1987). Substance over style: Assessing the efficacy of modality testing and teaching. *Exceptional Children*.

Koller, D., Andrew Ng, Chuong Do, and Zhenghao Chen. (2013). Retention and Intention in Massive Open Online Courses: *In Depth Educause Review* 03.06.13 Available at: http://www.educause.edu/ero/article/retention-and-intention-massive-open-online-courses-depth-0 (Accessed 10.04.20).

Konnikova, M. (2014). Will MOOCs be Flukes, *The New Yorker* 07.11.14 available at: http://www.newyorker.com/science/maria-konnikova/moocs-failure-solutions (Accessed 10.04.20).

Landmark. (2015). www.landmarkworldwide.com/ *(Accessed 10.04.20).*

Mazur, E. (1998). *Peer Instruction*: A User's Manual. Eaglewood Cliffs, NJ: Prentice-Hall.

McLeod, S. (2007). "Pavlov's Dogs." *Simply Psychology*. Available at: http://www.simplypsychology.org/pavlov.html (Accessed 22.02.21).

Meyer, D. L. (2009). 'The Poverty of Constructivism.' *Educational Philosophy and Theory,* 41(3), 332-341.

Motley, M. T. (1997). *Overcoming Your Fear of Public Speaking – A Proven Method* Boston: Houghton Mifflin Company ISBN: 0-395-88459-4.

Osgood, C. O. (Ed.) (1917). *Boswell's Life of Johnson* (abridged) Available online at: http://www.classic-literature.co.uk/scottish-authors/james-boswell/life-of-johnson-abridged/ebook-page-195.asp (Accessed 08.04.20).

Oxford Dictionaries. *Oxford Dictionaries Online.* (2011) available at: http://www.oxforddictionaries.com/definition/english/lecture (Accessed 08.04.20).

Pappanonov, L. (2012). The Year of the MOOC *The New York Times* 02.11.12 http://www.nytimes.com/2012/11/04/education/edlife/massive-open-online-courses-are-multiplying-at-a-rapid-pace.html?pagewanted=all&_r=0 (Accessed 10.04.20).

Perna, L., et al. "The life cycle of a million MOOC users." *Presentation at the MOOC Research Initiative Conference.* 2013. Available at:

http://www.gse.upenn.edu/pdf/ahead/perna_ruby_boruch_moocs_dec2 013.pdf Penn Study 2013 (Accessed 10.04.20).

Ross, A. (2000). *Curriculum Construction and Critique Oxford: Routledge.* Oxford: Routledge. p. 34-35.

Schneider, R. U. (2008). *The Mad Science Book: 100 Amazing Experiments from the history of Science Quercus Publishing Plc.* Youtube, (uploaded 13.06.11), clip available at: https://www.youtube.com/watch? v=RcxW6nrWwtc (Accessed 10.04.20).

Schulte, P. L. (1996). A definition of constructivism. *Science Scope*, 20(3), 25-27.

Skinner, B. F. (1954). *The science of learning and the art of teaching.* Cambridge, Mass, USA, 99-113.

Yamane, D. (2006). *Concept Preparation Assignments: a strategy for creating discussion-based course, Teaching Sociology,* 34:236-48.

In: The Impact of COVID-19 on Teaching …   ISBN: 978-1-53619-947-5
Editors: S. Studente, S. Ellis et al.   © 2021 Nova Science Publishers, Inc.

Chapter 8

HOW HAS COVID-19 SHIFTED HOW WE SUPPORT, RECOGNISE AND MEASURE STUDENT ENGAGEMENT?

Rachel C. Bassett-Dubsky[*], *EdD*
Faculty of Health, Education and Society,
University of Northampton, Northampton, United Kingdom

ABSTRACT

Throughout the 2019-2020 academic year, the engagement, achievement and progression of a level 4 cohort at a post-92 university in the East of England were explored in collaboration with the student cohort; questioning measurements of engagement (Bassett-Dubsky, 2020). Even before COVID-19, students recognised the performative function of such measures.

This chapter suggests that available indicators of student engagement have not been fit for purpose during lockdown and online learning and have exposed issues with existing measurements. Pre-lockdown, students in this study viewed both attendance and meeting submission deadlines as a matter for individual choice, such that neither factor may directly indicate engagement. During lockdown, students might engage in a recorded taught

---

[*] Corresponding Author's E-mail: Rachel.Bassett-Dubsky@northampton.ac.uk.

session at a time of their individual choosing in ways that support greater engagement but are measured as non-attendance - equated with non-engagement. During COVID, we have appreciated that absence or premature departure may be due to a range of issues, including digital exclusion (Yates, 2020), lack of space at home for work, and inconvenience of session time given lockdown-related responsibilities. If we can be flexible in our interpretation and support of engagement that is not signalled by attendance during COVID, we can continue to be so post-COVID. Similarly, rapid embrace of lecture capture and technology-enabled inclusive pedagogy have brought positives to lockdown learning we may wish to retain, although the role of learner analytics is considered more sceptically.

Pre-COVID, the factor seen by the study cohort as most indicative of student engagement was, 'Determination to progress and achieve'. This chapter suggests that lockdown has altered how we might identify whether a student is determined to progress and achieve, and how we might better appreciate barriers to acting on that determination. This chapter recommends that HEI should retain the Inclusive flexibilities of lockdown learning (Wonkhe & Aula, 2021) that allow student personalisation and extend these flexibilities to our interpretation and recognition (Wong and Chiu, 2020) of subjective student engagements (Parkes et al., 2020).

Keywords: student engagement, Inclusion, attendance, participation

INTRODUCTION

Student engagement is a contentious construct that lacks consensus of definition (Venn et al., 2020), yet wields considerable power (Bunce et al., 2021; Zepke, 2018). Digital traces, or 'touch points' (de Freitas et al., 2015), are over-relied upon to make behaviourally-driven normative value judgements of students' engagement within systems that are not yet inclusive enough to support the diversity of widened participation. Performative pressures to evidence practice that supports participation increase reliance on background and behavioural data but act against enabling that participation by rendering individual complexities (and anything not objectively measurable) invisible.

Significant changes to practice and interactions during COVID-19 have shown that the legitimacy of many of our pre-COVID interpretations of behaviour cannot be attributed to meaningful engagement as was once claimed. During COVID, staff have been willing and able to embrace new and more flexible ways of working (Wonkhe and Aula, 2021), which can be seen to offer real opportunity for better inclusive practice post-COVID.

WHAT IS ENGAGEMENT AND HOW IS IT ASSESSED?

Engagement is seen as the 'primary construct' when we look at student retention and progression (Korhonen et al., 2019). It cannot be reduced to a simplistic equation and must consider multiple, shifting, complex and diverse internal and external factors that shape what is possible, desirable and observable in subjective engagements (Zepke, 2018). The multiplicities of students' experience, however, are missed by the grand narratives so often driving engagement discourse and the 'big data' informing it (Gravett, Kinchin and Winstone, 2020). Korhonen (2012, p. 297) seeks to recognise a more holistic student experience and defines engagement as, "the level of integration of students in their studying environment". One of the key indicators of engagement is Attendance (Benkwitz et al., 2019), which is seen as critical to student success (Moores, Birdi and Higson, 2019) and easily measurable (perhaps part of why it is so key). However, assumptions that success is evidenced by absence of failure (Archer and Prinsloo, 2020, p890) risks reading attendance as the absence of 'absent', where attendance is not synonymous with 'present'. Attendance facilitates evidencing of participation, which is seen across the literature as a particularly significant indicator of engagement. This is especially true of those with more community-based values who align greater participation with greater belonging (Korhonen et al., 2017) – a commonly agreed central dimension of engagement, alongside that of identity (Korhonen et al., 2019).

How we measure success and engagement is very much informed by who we envisage as our ideal learner (Broughan and Prinsloo, 2020). This identity is often constructed through a combination of traditional norms and what we can measure (Dyment, Stone and Milthorpe, 2020; Gravett, Kinchin and Winstone, 2020). If who we envisage as our ideal student is based on our own profile, given the lack of diversity in academia we risk reproducing discourses and expectations that are classed, gendered and raced (Wong and Chiu, 2020).

Discourse around engagement "embraces dominant ideas about knowledge, performativity, accountability and the very purposes of higher education" (Zepke, 2018, p439). Government discourse has constructed the 'ideally engaged learner' based on a transactional exchange such that students are "units of systemic growth" that must show return on investment (Kelly et al., 2017, p106). This functional and reductive construct is too singular and impersonal to engage with, or be inclusive of, the complexities of student diversity.

The concept of the ideal learner is relevant in that it seems consistent with student engagement discourse that situates the responsibility for engagement in and with the student, as if any fault or responsibility is theirs. Gourley (2017, p. 23) refers to views of 'student engagement' as relating to what is desirable "in students" so that HEI teaching might be seen as successful. If this is re-phrased as 'interactions desired from and with a student by the university', the responsibility seems like more of a joint endeavour and makes it clear who is measuring and assessing those interactions (i.e., the university).

Exploring the Relative Value of Factors of Engagement with a Level 4 Cohort

There is a lack of consensus about which dimensions of student engagement are of most value, who they are valued by, and how they are promoted (Kelly et al., 2017; Venn et al., 2020). Much of the discourse is driven from a behavioural perspective, which tallies with the quantitative nature of the majority of the research around measurement of 'engagement' (Moores, Birdi and Higson, 2019). However, defining student engagement from this perspective lacks clarity and is limited by the nature of the data on which it is based, such that it offers little understanding of the individual students whose engagement it judges (Kahu, 2013, p. 760). Such an approach seems to be driven by availability of data (Bond et al., 2020), such that we value what we measure – not because it is inherently valuable but because we can (Kelly et al., 2017; MacFarlane & Tomlinson, 2017; Dyment, Stone and Milthorpe, 2020)

Throughout the 2019-2020 academic year, the engagements, achievement and progression of a level 4 cohort at a post-92 university in the East of England were explored in collaboration with the student cohort; questioning measurements of engagement (Bassett-Dubsky, 2020)[1]. Focus groups based on a Diamond-9 ranking activity of factors that indicate engagement showed that what students agreed was most indicative of engagement was 'Determination to progress and achieve'. Of all the available factors, this was the hardest (most subjective) for the university to recognise; what students found most meaningful was least measurable. 'Determination...' could be seen as the antecedent to the engagement – "the intent and unobservable force that energises behaviour" (Bond et al., 2020, p. 3), which would lead to the following definition of engagement: 'Determination to progress and achieve leading to actions that constructively support that determination'.

When asked how tutors might recognise this determination, it was through deduction based on seeing they had engaged with; "Wider research" and were "communicating" and "coming to lessons with more knowledge" as well as having to "just overhear" and "gauge" it. These clues would be easy to miss and rely on tutors being in the right place at the right time, equitably, and interpreting what they were hearing and gauging equitably. "Coming to lessons" suggests attendance is a pre-requisite for these inference/performance opportunities. "Wider Research" might be indicated by digital traces of library loans and e-resource access, but there are so many opportunities for relevant wider research that would not be captured. It was interesting that none of the focus groups suggested the way to find out how determined a student might be to progress and achieve was to ask them. Fuller et al. (2018) found that students were pretending to engage for 23% of session time, even where the tutor was rated highly. Their desire to be

---

[1] Further details from throughout the project may be found on the project blog (see references).

seen as engaging was partly to avoid offence to the tutor and partly to avoid getting into trouble (*Op Cit*, p19). This may suggest our visible reading of attendance as engagement leads to behaviours that are both performative and infantilising (MacFarlane and Tomlinson, 2017). It also reinforces the unreliability of interpretation of engagement on the basis of observation (Fuller et al., 2018).

We are increasingly operating in a culture of presenteeism, where attending and engaging are very different things (MacFarlane, 2012, p. 27). Attending but not being present (playing games or looking at social media on a phone, chatting off topic with friends, sat there quietly whilst being somewhere else in your mind) was seen by the study cohort as an empty presence and therefore meaningless in terms of indicating engagement. Presence and participation must be meaningful if engagement is to be meaningful (Korhonen, 2012). The study group did value attendance as an aid to learning and saw its benefit for interaction (and improved communication) that would support learning and achievement. There were clear echoes of 'the Index for Inclusion' (Booth and Ainscow, 2002) in these themes, in that Presence, Participation and Achievement were all closely linked and needed to all be active for meaningful engagement.

Looking at student engagements within a narrative of Inclusion helps re-frame engagement discourse to focus on barriers to engagement and how they might be removed (Korhonen, 2012, p. 297) more than on how to perform engagement. This also shifts more of the responsibility for student engagement towards the university. However, ironically, it is probably the pressures of evidencing meeting that responsibility that lead to an over-focus on behavioural measures of engagement, since they deliver more certainty – at the cost of participating in technologies of control (Zepke, 2015).

The Role of Learner/Learning Analytics and Digital Traces

With an awareness of the unreliability of observation as the basis for interpretation of engagement in class and tasks (Fuller et al., 2018), learner/learning analytics (LA) may offer greater objectivity and scope in what they measure. LA pull contextual data and digital traces from different systems into one, where they may be presented through a visual dashboard. As part of a growing emphasis on the process of learning, LA are able to capture indicators of presence and participation, as well as more conventional measures of achievement (MacFarlane & Tomlinson, 2017, p. 12). This may bring opportunities to supportively intervene in relation to presence and participation, with a view to improving achievement. However, it risks pressurising students into complying with what their setting thinks learning should look like (Bunce et al., 2021; Broughan and Prinsloo, 2020) when we need to recognise that there is more than one way to be a good learner. Students need to be allowed to work in their own way to feel included in their studies (Tobbell et al., 2021).

We need to remember that LA should serve us, rather than us serving it (i.e., avoid tailoring what we do to what it can measure). For example, if we look to use LA for additional indicators of participation, this may lead us to create 'busy work' in order to evidence participation, but does not indicate engagement in anything of value (Dyment, Stone and Milthorpe, 2020). An example of such 'busy work' might be an online discussion board to which students are required to post a certain number of times and respond to a set number of posts from their peers. Where this happens without any tutor interaction or personalised feedback, it is not perceived as valuable by students, despite being conveniently measurable (Op Cit). 'Busy work' may even obstruct engagement by taking time away from more meaningful activities (Op Cit), as well as conveying to students that it is compliance with tutor-set activities that counts as 'engagement' and therefore that are of value – disempowering them as agentic learners (Kahu, 2013; Broughan and Prinsloo, 2020). There is a crucial difference between 'being engaged' and engaging with (participating in) a particular task. The latter is current-context and content dependent whilst the former is broader, more holistic and ongoing. LA measure what is engaged with, but not why or the value of that activity.

This leads to the concern that LA may be too reductive and fail to acknowledge individual complexities (Parkes et al., 2020) such that the potential efficiencies may ignore messy (yet highly relevant) issues of context (Benkwitz et al., 2019) and lead to attribution error in conflating the 'what' with the 'why' when all that is measured are proxies for learning (Archer and Prinsloo, 2020).

Not only is attribution error an interpretive risk, there is also risk of information overload through a vast and increasing array of data, that needs to be filtered and transformed into insights by someone who is context-aware (Foster and Siddle, 2020; Herodotou et al., 2019; Agudo-Peregrina et al., 2014). One way overload may be avoided is through specifically targeted use; perhaps prioritising particular digital traces (although which traces may be significant in which ways, and to what extent, is still contentious and unproven). An alternative is not to distinguish between the potential value of particular traces and look at the bigger picture of any digital interaction trace vs total non-interaction (Foster and Siddle, 2020). No engagement alerts that pick up a set time period without any digital trace and go directly to the relevant tutor for them to initiate contact with the student are claimed to create a background-neutral framework for interaction (Op cit, p. 852). This background neutrality is presented as a positive that avoids stereotype and stigma. However, the potential stigma comes from the response to the background, not the recognition and acknowledgement of that background. We need to know students through personal contact, as contextualised individuals, to develop the trust and rapport necessary for our students to feel they belong (Bunce et al., 2021). Additionally, if it takes three weeks from the start of term to trigger such an alert (and the subsequent interaction) this seems like valuable time lost, especially if engagement behaviours in the first three weeks correlate positively with more frequent digital traces and higher attainment throughout the course of study (Summers, Higson and Moores, 2020) and when we know that students want us to react to non-interaction (Moores, Birdi and Higson, 2019).

When we consider the scope of digital traces, we should be aware how broad this scope is and how the type of data collected differs between HEIs. Differing availability and reliability of data may lead to claims on the basis of what we have rather than what might be most insightful. Students in the Diamond-9 study cohort were aware that their HEI's LA dashboard captured the following: Attendance (through card swipes by the student in the classroom or manual addition by the tutor), VLE log-ins, Module log-ins within the VLE, Library loans[2], E-resource access (number of), Academic skills tutorials. These were then collated and fed back through the visual dashboard as overall engagement; using a traffic light system to indicate degrees of engagement and offering a comparative option for students to compare their engagement with the cohort average.

There is much potential limitation in the utility of these data (Summers, Higson and Moores, 2020). Frequency of log in to VLE only seems to correlate with outcome for online courses, not with face to face courses (Op Cit). Library use data only captures the numbers of times of access or loan – not how long that source was engaged with or whether it was read at all. It also misses entirely students who do not borrow the text but sit in the library to use it (Op Cit); or students who buy the text; or students who download a journal article once (one 'engagement credit' for library use) but then go on to read it multiple times or share it with a friend – who then gets no 'engagement credit' at all for their invisible source engagement; or students who access relevant academic material online but outside of the university library system. Attendance shows an 'engagement credit' for students who swiped in to a Face to Face session, or logged in online… regardless of what followed that initial swipe or log in. The engagement of students who do not attend in person but watch a lecture recording and engage with the session materials is not externally credited (captured in the dashboard), although lecture capture data is included in many systems. Students who study together outside of class (with such interactive participation often seen as valuable for attainment and belonging (Korhonen et al., 2017)) may work with one laptop between them, with one user logging in to the VLE and relevant module sites on behalf of the group – but only the engagement of the logged in user is visible in the digital trace. If students download the material they need from the VLE, they have reduced need for further logging on – and reduced opportunity therefore to evidence their engagement with those materials, because we are only looking for very particular signs of interaction as evidence of engagement.

---

[2] During the 2019-20 academic year, the Library loan feedthrough was not available.

During COVID-19

When we focus on measuring participation, we are aware that there are many reasons why a student may not participate consistently and reliably in discussions or learning activities. Teaching and learning during COVID-19 has increased the legitimacy (a value-judgement) of many of these reasons. Family, health and personal problems (Neves, 2019) have been widespread for the majority – not just for students. Anxiety, uncertainty, wellbeing, isolation and lack of motivation have been concerns across the HEI community (Dickinson, 2020; Wonkhe and Aula, 2021; Dodd et al., 2021). Childcare responsibilities have limited study time and which times are suitable for being online (Rainford, 2021), with 45% of respondents in some studies saying their home environment did not support online learning (Dodd et al., 2021).

HEI colleagues have seen both improvements and additional barriers to student engagement during COVID-19 (Wonkhe and Aula, 2021). Attendance in particular seems to have been a measure less fit for purpose, being both improved (in that students are present/logging in) but less meaningful (in that attendance is not leading to work completion or interaction) (Op cit).

Digital exclusion has created further barriers to engagement (Yates, 2020; Wonkhe and Aula, 2021) with the ONS impact study (2020, p. 5) finding that 16% of students did not feel equipped to engage with online learning. Dissatisfaction with online learning seemed driven, not by quality, but by difficulties accessing it and lack of Wifi (Dickinson, 2020), with over half of students having unreliable internet access that disrupted their learning (Dodd et al., 2021, p. 6). Inequity of access to technology is significant (Rainford, 2021) and we must ensure that other inequities of access are made equally visible.

During COVID-19, learning technologies were an essential enabler to support inclusivity and accessibility (Venn et al., 2020). The way learning resources were provided, courses were structured and assessed, and what guidance was given to students on how to spend their independent study time were all substantially changed (Wonkhe and Aula, 2021). HEI colleagues are both willing and able to adapt their approaches. Better inclusion for students with diverse backgrounds and life experiences has been explicitly recognised as a priority for post-pandemic practice (op cit) and our changed ways of working during COVID-19 have opened up opportunities for greater Inclusion.

In terms of how we measure and understand engagement, HEI colleagues' demand for better technology-driven insights (Wonkhe and Aula, 2021) suggest that what is currently captured is recognised as inadequate for the claims that are based upon it. COVID-19 practice has made default assumptions about how engagement is indicated by students' online behaviours and digital traces (Archer and Prinsloo, 2020) far less credible. This is largely because we all have first-hand experience of significant challenges and barriers throughout COVID. Therefore, it may be that interest convergence might lead to greater flexibility for students and staff (Bell, 1980; cited by Nishi, 2020, p. 2). Whilst this might effect change towards better Inclusion, motivation stemming from interest convergence is mostly temporary (Nishi, 2020) and we must ensure that what we have learnt during COVID-19 leads to enduring systemic change.

Transferability of Practice and System Gains during COVID to a Post-COVID Context

Gilardi and Guglielmetti (2011) flag the paradox of widening participation into a system that is insufficiently inclusive in its structure and practice. A diversity of students has not made Inclusion inevitable (Tobbell et al., 2021). We need to be more flexible in our HEI systems to support non-traditional students so that they might achieve, "balance between their academic and external commitments that enables them to reach a level of engagement sufficient to achieve academic success" (Gilardi & Guglielmetti, 2011, p. 36).

Even pre-COVID, a majority of students reported struggling with feelings of anxiety (Barkas et al., 2020, p7) and we know that significant further decline in mental health has been a widespread impact of the pandemic (ONS, 2020; Dodd et al., 2021). If we can support autonomy in our students, through our systems, this may help counter increasingly high levels of student anxiety and support the many students who report being overwhelmed (Barkas et al., 2020; Tobbell et al., 2021). This would mean giving students much more choice in how and when they learn and are assessed (Op Cit) so that they work in ways and environments that are empowering for them (Pearson et al., 2019).

We need to be flexible about "where, when, how and with whom learning takes place" (Kelly et al. 2017, p. 117). During COVID-19 we have seen that HEI communities can both do and value this flexible approach (Wonkhe and Aula, 2021). If we can agree that factors like attendance and meeting submission deadlines might be supportive of engagement, whilst not directly indicating engagement, might that change the way that we label and use such data? This might include retention of multiple submission windows that were part of some HEI emergency regulations during the first lockdown, allowing student choice of when to make first submission from numerous possible opportunities. If we are looking to be proactive and support people to be mentally healthy rather than being reactive (Korhonen, 2012) we need to give them more agency to manage their workload (including assignment submissions) proactively, rather than wait until they are in distress in order to become eligible for mitigation (Barkas et al., 2020). The multiple submission windows supported student agency whilst removing the need for formal mitigation bureaucracy (Kettell, 2018). The deficit model of student engagement suggests issues with meeting deadlines that are published at the start of the academic year are due to poor time management on the part of the student, and the advance notice of the deadlines should facilitate students to manage their time adequately. However, "students do not seem to find this practice enabling" (Tobbell et al., p. 291). There were system challenges in ensuring smooth progression and enrolment onto subsequent level modules (as well as managing less predictable marking loads). However, these are system issues (that hard-working colleagues overcame so that progression and enrolment were possible) and the system should serve the people. If we can overcome such vast systemic challenges under such time pressures during a global pandemic, surely, we can retain the benefits of those changes and make their administration smoother post-COVID.

When we consider factors like attendance and meeting submission deadlines, we need to recognise also that they are related. In presenting both measures as indicative of engagement, and making the nature of both fixed and inflexible, we could be working at cross-purposes. The most cited reason for student non-attendance is other university commitments, where nearly half of all absences were due to students doing other work for their course (Oldfield et al., 2018, p. 515; Moores, Birdi and Higson, 2019, p. 379). These students were engaged with their studies, but they were not enabled by the system within which they were working to maximise or fully evidence that engagement. Inclusive flexibilities should allow students space to evidence the necessary learning outcomes and quality standards in the way that is best for them (Tobbell et al., 2021).

Similarly, our expectations of what engaged attendance looks like, and what might impact on the nature of attendance, have shifted. If "it does not matter *if* but rather how students attend class" (Buchele, 2021, p. 132) then to maximise meaningful attendance we should provide multiple ways for students to attend to their learning – online (live), face to face, online asynchronous, a combination of these options; a student-led choice on a session by session basis. Flexible practice enables participation (Tobbell et al., 2021) whereas a stubborn requirement for face to face attendance as a singular mode of engagement makes it difficult for many students to engage at all (Thomas, 2020, p. 297).

We know that more flexible practice in relation to forms of attendance would ease the particular pressures experienced by many 'non-traditional' students, including young carers (Kettell, 2018), students with mental health difficulties (Barkas et al., 2020; Tobbell et al., 2021), commuter students (Gravett, Kinchin and Winstone, 2020; Thomas, 2020), students from minoritised ethnicities (Bunce et al., 2021), students with dyslexia (Dommett et al., 2019), students with English as an additional language (Caglayan and Ustunluoglu, 2021). If we continue to employ more Inclusive approaches to effective pedagogy (Tobbell et al., 2021) and what we interpret as presence and participation, we will benefit all students (Pearson et al., 2019).

We might measure the impact of presence and participation through achievement, but our measurement of achievement must then be individualised. Effort cannot be objectively assessed (if visible at all), yet it is an attribute of the 'ideal student' that outweighs any resultant achievement level (Wong and Chiu, 2020). If we interpret outcome for effort, we may unfairly judge and demotivate students who perceive their effort as unseen (Bunce et al., 2021). A grade of C might be well-received and good progress for one student yet B+ might be perceived as disastrous and off-track for another (Bunce et al., 2021). The focus on (and definition of) 'good grades' as 2:1 or higher seems damaging to students' sense of competence. Likewise, assessing 'graduate employability' as a higher attainment risks reinforcing the 'return on investment' transactional construct of 'engagement' (Kelly et al., 2017) and ignores how most of the key roles in many subject areas are not seen as graduate roles.

The Role of Learner/Learning Analytics Post-COVID

Our use of LA also needs to evolve. Interpretation and use of LA must recognise diverse and individual experience and any use of LA must be learner centred (Archer and Prinsloo, 2020) and genuinely collaborative with students (Parkes et al., 2020, p113). We should define and understand categories and concepts relating to student engagement with students (Foster and Francis, 2020) and move away from interpretations based on deficit models (Broughan and Prinsloo, 2020). This can only be done through ongoing conversation with individual students.

Unless student agency (Broughan and Prinsloo, 2020, p619) drives our use of LA, raising students' awareness of LA might both disempower (Broughan and Prinsloo, 2020, p. 625) and increase performativity (Bassett-Dubsky, 2020) which could then lead students to disengage (Kahu, 2013, p. 763). It may even decrease students' mastery goal orientation (Lonn, Aguilar and Teasley, 2015), along with correlated cognitive engagement (Korhonen et al., 2019), whilst reinforcing a consumer model of Higher Education. It is vital that we focus our efforts on how we use LA at an individual level (Herodotou et al., 2019).

Multiple sources suggest that the most effective and inclusive way to meaningfully understand and support student engagement is through relationships - personalised student-tutor interactions (Tobbell et al., 2021; Agudo-Peregrina et al., 2014; Summers, Higson and Moores, 2020). Tutors who are already more engaged with their students seem to have students with better learning outcomes (Herodotou et al., 2019). Students want more interaction with their tutors, though many may be shy to initiate that interaction (Yale, 2019) or have adopted sub-optimal 'coping alone' strategies (Bunce et al., 2021). Where use of LA can instigate and better inform student-tutor interaction, such that tutors might ask better questions; this would help us better understand what is happening behind the 'touch-point' data (de Freitas et al., 2015). Arguably, LA is not necessary to build these relationships or ask these questions. If the argument for LA is that it helps us ask better questions more efficiently through targeting students at risk, because tutors in pastoral roles have only minimal time allocated to that role (Tobbell et al., 2021; Foster and Siddle, 2020), then the issue is with the time allocated that causes LA to be used non-inclusively. Every student should be able to benefit from relationship-building and data-informed conversations with a tutor (Yale, 2019).

Lecture Recordings Post-COVID

Finally, increased availability of lecture recordings during COVID-19 has been well received and should continue. Lecture capture seems to empower student choice and flexibility with little impact on their attainment (Moores, Birdi and Higson, 2019). It facilitates autonomy in students' learning and the pace of learning and is valued by students such that it increases student satisfaction ratings (Dommett et al., 2019). Even just knowing that the recordings are there acts as a safety net that students value and find reassuring (Op Cit). Whether the format of the lecture recording was live-streamed or pre-recorded, the vast majority of students who report using the recordings found them very helpful to their learning (Witton, 2016). Lecture recordings are most effective when they are used in conjunction with live session attendance, when they can actually decrease the risk of student's dropping out (de Freitas et al., 2015) – re-engaging students who might otherwise be non-attaining and read as non-engaged. Frequent users of lecture recordings are more likely to have dyslexia or be non-native speakers of English (Caglayan and Ustunluogu, 2021), who need that supportive opportunity to self-pace and re-play key parts of a session.

There are potential issues for students with lecture capture. We would want to avoid students being lulled into a false sense of security in thinking that use of recorded lectures alone is as effective for learning as attending a live session (Dommett et al., 2019). Much student use of lecture recordings involves watching only very short selections from the whole session, such that just accessing the recording does not equate to engaging with the session as a whole (Caglayan and Ustunluogu, 2021). As with any resource, we would have to make it accessible and clearly navigable, as well as discussing how it might best be utilised.

There are also potential issues with lecture capture for academics. Wonkhe and Aula (2021) flag concerns that embracing a more blended approach could be seen as a cost-cutting opportunity, where recorded lectures might be re-used without need for the creating academic. If we are to build improvement into our post-COVID practice that embraces these inclusive opportunities, there needs to be much better trust between staff who teach and support and those in higher management (Op cit) such that we can trust we are not working ourselves out of employment. This is particularly true in a context where HEI finances are constrained and increased redundancies are visible (Fazackerley, 2021; Petrescu, 2021). If we are doing live lectures we are needed; If use of lecture recordings is increased (and previous recordings re-used) then it is not only the lecture that no longer needs to be live (Basken, 2021).

CONCLUSION

We need to be able to recognise the benefits and opportunities of digitally enabled practice whilst also staying aware that digital exclusion remains an issue. Giving students agency to navigate a more flexible system with a variety of engagement options would allow them to make the best decisions for themselves, as necessary within their current and evolving contexts. We also need to recognise that greater flexibility is likely to free students from our digital overview and mean that we will only know much of what they might do to engage by asking them. These changes will allow for multiple ways of being a good learner that may, in turn, reduce performativity. Once the pressure of compliance with a single model is removed, our best option for understanding and supporting student engagement will continue to be direct and personalised conversation with individual students. Space for these conversations needs to be facilitated in workload planning to support all students to be present, participate and achieve.

REFERENCES

Agudo-Peregrina, A., Iglesias-Pradas, S., Conde-Gonzalez, M. and Hernandez-Garcia, A. (2014). 'Can we predict success from log data in VLEs? Classification of interactions for learning analytics and their relation with performance in VLE-supported F2F and online learning', *Computers in Human Behavior,* 31, pp 542-550.

Archer, E. and Prinsloo, P. (2020). 'Speaking the unspoken in learning analytics: troubling the defaults', *Assessment & Evaluation in Higher Education,* 45(6), pp 888-900.

Barkas, L., Armstrong, P-A, and Bishop, G. (2020). 'Is Inclusion still an illusion in higher education? Exploring the curriculum through the student voice', *International Journal of Inclusive Education,* DOI: 10.1080/13603116.2020.1776777.

Basken, P. (2021). Dead professor's course alerts faculty to COVID-era rights. *Times Higher Education.* Available from: https://www.time shighereducation.com/search?e=404&search=news%20dead%20profes sors%20course%20alerts%20faculty%20COVID%20era%20rights%2 0on%2008%2004%2021.

Bassett-Dubsky, R. (2020). *Student engagements project blog*, (January update –Focus group analysis) https://mypad.northampton.ac.uk/ rdubsk/.

Benkwitz, A., Parkers, S., Bardy, H., Myler, K., Peters, J., Akhtar, A., Keeling, P., Preece, R. and Smith, T. (2019). 'Using student data: Student-staff collaborative development of compassionate pedagogic interventions based on learning analytics and mentoring', *Journal of Hospitality, Leisure, Sport & Tourism Education,* 25.

Bond, M., Buntins, K., Bedenlier, S., Zawacki-Richter, O. and Kerres, M. (2020). 'Mapping research in student engagement and educational technology in higher education: a systematic evidence map', *International Journal of Educational Technology in Higher Education,* 17(2).

Booth, T. and Ainscow, M. (2002). *Index for Inclusion: developing learning and participation in schools.* Center for Studies on Inclusive Education (CSIE) Accessed at https://www.eenet.org.uk/resources/docs/Index %20English.pdf on 04/01/20.

Broughan, C. and Prinsloo, P. (2020). '(Re)centring students in learning analytics: in conversation with Paulo Freire', *Assessment & Evaluation in Higher Education,* 45(1), pp617-628.

Buchele, S. (2021). 'Evaluating the link between attendance and performance in higher education: the role of classroom engagement dimensions', *Assessment & Evaluation in Higher Education,* 46(1), pp132-150.

Bunce, L., King, N., Saran, S. and Talib, N. (2021). 'Experiences of black and minority ethnic (BME) students in higher education: applying self-determination theory to understand the BME attainment gap', *Studies in Higher Education,* 46(3), pp534-547.

Caglayan, E. and Ustunluoglu, E. (2021). 'A Study exploring Students' Usage Patterns and Adoption of Lecture Capture', *Technology, Knowledge and Learning*, 26, pp13-30.

Dickinson, J. (2020). *The Costs of COVID restrictions on students are social*, Accessed at https://wonkhe.com/blogs/anti-social-learning-the-costs-of-COVID-restrictions-on-students/ on 05/11/20.

Dodd, R., Dadaczynski, K., Okan, O., McCaffery, K. and Pickles, K. (2021). 'Psychological Wellbeing and Academic Experience of University Students in Australia during COVID-19', *International Journal of Environmental Research and Public Health*, 16, pp866-877.

Dommett, E., Gardner, B. and van Tilburg, W. (2019). 'Staff and student views of lecture capture: a qualitative study', *International Journal of Educational Technology in Higher Education*, 16(23).

Dyment, J., Stone C. and Milthorpe, N. (2020). 'Beyond busy work: rethinking the measurement of online student engagement', *Higher Education Research & Development*, DOI: 10.1080/07294360. 2020.1732879.

Fazackerley, A (2021). *Despicable in a pandemic: fury as UK universities plan job cuts.* Available from: https://www.theguardian.com/ education/2021/jan/22/despicable-in-a-pandemic-fury-as-10-uk-universities-plan-job-cuts.

Foster, C. and Francis, P. (2020). 'A systematic review on the deployment and effectiveness of data analytics in higher education to improve student outcomes', *Assessment & Evaluation in Higher Education*, 45(6), pp822-841.

Foster, E. and Siddle, R. (2020). 'The effectiveness of learning analytics for identifying at-risk students in higher education', *Assessment & Evaluation in Higher Education*, 45(6), pp842-854.

Francis, P., Broughan, C., Foster, C. and Wilson, C. (2020). 'Thinking critically about learning analytics, student outcomes, and equity of attainment', *Assessment & Evaluation in Higher Education*, 45(6), pp811-821.

De Frietas, S., Gibson, D., Du Plessis, C., Halloran, P., Williams, E., Ambrose, M., Dunwell, I and Arnab, S. (2015). 'Foundations of dynamic learning analytics: Using university student data to increase retention', *British Journal of Educational Technology*, 46(6), pp1175-1188.

Fuller, K., Karunaratne, N., Naidu, S., Exintaris, B., Short, J., Wolcott, D., Singleton, S. and White, P. (2018). 'Development of a self-report instrument for measuring in-class student engagement reveals that pretending to engage is a significant unrecognized problem', *PLoS ONE* 13 (10): e0205828 https://doi.org/10.1371/journal.pone.0205828.

Gilardi, S. & Guglielmetti, C. (2011). 'University Life of Non-Traditional Students: Engagement Styles and Impact on Attrition', *The Journal of Higher Education*, 82(1), pp33-53.

Gourlay, L. (2017). 'Student Engagement, 'Learnification' and the Sociomaterial: Critical Perspectives on Higher Education Policy', *Higher Education Policy*, 30, pp23-34.

Gravett, K., Kinchin, I. and Winstone, N. (2020). 'Frailty in transition? Troubling the norms, boundaries and limitations of transition theory and practice', *Higher Education Research & Development*, 39(6), pp1169-1185.

Herodotou, C., Rienties, B., Boroowa, A., Zdrahal, Z. and Hlosta, M. (2019). 'A large-scale implementation of predictive learning analytics in higher education: the teachers' role and perspective', *Education Teach Research Dev*, 67, pp1273-1306.

Kahu, E. (2013). 'Framing student engagement in higher education', *Studies in Higher Education*, 38(5), pp758-773.

Kelly. P, Fair. N and Evans, C (2017). 'The Engaged Student ideal in Higher Education Policy', *Higher Education Policy*, 30, pp105-122.

Kettell, L. (2018). 'Young adult carers in higher education: the motivations, barriers and challenges involved – a UK study', *Journal of Further and Higher Education*, DOI: 10.1080/0309877X.2018.1515427.

Korhonen, V. (2012). 'Towards Inclusive Higher Education? – Outlining a Student-centred Counselling Framework for Strengthening Student Engagement' in S. Stolz & P. Gonon (eds.) (2012) *Challenges and Reforms in Vocational Education - Aspects of Inclusion and Exclusion*. Bern: Peter Lang, 297-320.

Korhonen, V., Inkinen, M., Mattsson, M. and Toom, A. (2017). 'Student engagement and the transition from the first to second year in higher education', In *Higher Education Transitions: Theory and Research*, eds E. Kyndt, et al. (London: Routledge), 113–134.

Korhonen, V., Mattsson, M., Inkinen, M. and Toom, A. (2019). 'Understanding the multidimensional nature of Student Engagement during the first year of Higher Education', *Frontiers in Psychology*, 10(1056), pp1-15.

Lonn, S., Aguialr, A., and Teasley, A. (2015). 'Investigating student motivation in the context of a learning analytics intervention during a summer bridge program', *Computers in Human Behavior*, 47, pp90-97.

MacFarlane, B. (2012) 'Be here now, or else: lamentable effects of student 'presenteeism', *Times Higher Education*, p26-27.

MacFarlane, B. and Tomlinson, M. (2017). 'Critiques of Student Engagement', *Higher Education Policy*, 30, pp5-21.

Moores, E., Birdi, G. and Higson, H. (2019). 'Determinants of university students' attendance', *Educational Research*, 61(4), pp371-387.

Neves, J. (2019). *UK Engagement Survey. Advance HE*. Accessible at https://www.advance-he.ac.uk/reports-publications-and-resources/student-surveys/uk-engagement-survey-ukes [Accessed on 8th June 2020].

Nishi, N. (2020). 'Imperialistic reclamation of higher education diversity initiatives through semantic co-option and concession', *Race Ethnicity and Education*, DOI:10.1080/13613324.2020.1718079.

Oldfield, J., Rodwell, J., Curry, L. and Marks, G. (2018). 'Psychological and demographic predictors of undergraduate non-attendance at university lectures and seminars', *Journal of Further and Higher Education*, 42(4), pp509-523.

ONS (2020). *Coronavirus and the impact on students in higher education in England: September to December 2020*, Accessed at https://www.ons.gov.uk/peoplepopulationandcommunity/educationandchildcare/articles/coronavirusandtheimpactonstudentsinhighereducationinenglandseptembertodecember2020/2020-12-21 on 08/01/2021.

Parkes, S., Benkwitz, A., Bardy, H., Myler, K., Peters, J. (2020). 'Being more human: rooting learning analytics through resistance and reconnection with the values of higher education', *Higher Education Research and Development* 39(1), pp113-126.

Pearson, V., Lister, K., McPherson, E., Gallen, A-M., Davies, G., Colwell, C., Bradshaw, K., Brathwaite, N and Collins, T. (2019). 'Embvedding and Sustaining Inclusive Practice to Support Disabled Students in Online and Blended Learning', *Journal of Interactive Media in Education*, 1(4).

Petrescu, I (2021). *UK universities and colleges escalate attacks on jobs and pay as Johnson government reopens unsafe campuses.* Available from: https://www.wsws.org/en/articles/2021/03/10/unuk-m10.html.

Rainford, J. (2021). 'Moving widening participation outreach online: challenge or opportunity?', Perspectives: *Policy and Practice in Higher Education*, 25(1), pp2-6.

Summers, R., Higson, H. and Moores, E. (2020). 'Measures of engagement in the first three weeks of higher education predict subsequent activity and attainment in first year undergraduate students: a UK case study', *Assessment & Evaluation in Higher Education*, DOI: 10.1080/02602938.2020.1822282.

Thomas, L. (2020). 'I am happy just doing the work… Commuter student engagement in the wider higher education experience', *Higher Education Quarterly*, 74, pp290-303.

Tobbell, J., Burton, R., Gaynor, A., Golding, B., Greenhough, K., Rhodes, C. and White, S. (2021). 'Inclusion in higher education: an exploration of the subjective experiences of students', *Journal of Further and Higher Education*, 45(2), pp284-295.

Venn, E., Park, J., Palle Anderson, L. and Hejmadi, M. (2020). 'How do learning technologies impact on undergraduates' emotional and cognitive engagement with their learning?', *Teaching in Higher Education*, DOI: 10.1080/13562517.2020.1863349.

Witton, G. (2017). 'The value of capture: Taking an alternative approach to using lecture capture technologies for increased impact on student learning and engagement', *British Journal of Educational Technology*, 48(4), pp1010-1019.

Wong, B. and Chiu, Y. (2020). 'University lecturer's construction of the 'ideal' undergraduate student', *Journal of Further and Higher Education*, 44(1), pp54-68.

Wonkhe and Aula (2021). *University staff experience of digitally enabled learning during COVID-19*, Full report accessed at https://wonkhe. com/blogs/educators-experience-of-digitally-enabled-learning-and-teaching-during-COVID-19/ on 15/03/21.

Yale. A. (2019). 'Quality matters: an in-depth exploration of the student–personal tutor relationship in higher education from the student perspective', *Journal of Further and Higher Education*, DOI: 10.1080/0309877X.2019.1596235.

Yates, S. (2020). Policy briefing 031: *COVID-19 and Digital Exclusion: Insights and Implications for the Liverpool City Region*, Accessed at https://www.liverpool.ac.uk/media/livacuk/publicpolicyamppractice/C OVID-19/Policy,Brief,031.pdf on 06/01/21.

Zepke, N. (2015). 'Student engagement research: thinking beyond the mainstream', *Higher Education Research & Development*, 34(6), pp1311-1323.

Zepke, N. (2018). 'Student engagement in neo-liberal times: what is missing?', *Higher Education Research & Development*, 37(2), pp433-446.

In: The Impact of COVID-19 on Teaching …   ISBN: 978-1-53619-947-5
Editors: S. Studente, S. Ellis et al.   © 2021 Nova Science Publishers, Inc.

Chapter 9

THE IMPACT OF COVID-19 ON STUDENT ENGAGEMENT AND EXPERIENCE

Bhavini Desai [*], PhD

Regent's University London, London, United Kingdom

ABSTRACT

Global spread of the COVID-19 pandemic has severely affected higher education, as universities closed their premises and countries shut their borders in response to lockdown measures. This crisis affected the continuity of learning and delivery of education. It has also affected international students and altered their perception of the value of their degree. International students were particularly affected at the start of the lockdown as they had to face the implications of university closures. Students had to make a choice on whether to return home with limited information about when they might return, or remain in their host country with restricted employment and education opportunities, all while sorting out their visa status. This further overflowed into their expectations from their respective academic institutions, their engagement with their tutors and peers and most importantly, severely altered their experiences.

In response to the need for providing a seamless learning experience and supporting tutors during this transition, in March 2020, a cross-

---

[*] Corresponding Author's E-mail: DesaiB@regents.ac.uk.

institutional approach at Regents University London (RUL) led to the establishment of the RADAR framework. The acronym RADAR refers to five broad learning activities: Research, Acquire, Discuss, Action, Reflect. These five verbs describe what is expected from all tutors and students regularly as part of a distinctive Regent's experience. In developing the RADAR framework, attention was turned to how this could work for all modules in a remote setting. The intention of the framework was to work towards fulfilling expectations by providing a more engaging experience.

This chapter discusses the struggles of adjusting to moving education online, followed by a discussion on understanding student engagement and expectations. The RADAR development and steps involved is outlined, followed by a discussion on how this affected the delivery, assessment, and engagement within modules.

The intention of this chapter is to understand the impact of the RADAR model on student engagement and experiences in online learning, concluding with an evaluation of the outcome of the process. Lessons learnt about how this learning can be carried into the future in order to improve student engagement and experience are presented as a conclusion.

Keywords: engagement, student experience, higher education

INTRODUCTION

The spread of COVID-19 has sent shockwaves across the globe. This public health crisis, unprecedented in our lifetimes, has caused severe human suffering and loss of life. It has challenged the way of life and altered the normal. We now live in what's called the 'new normal'. Some of the most common words of 2020 were; social distancing, lockdown, quarantine, and remote working. During this period, everyone stopped where they were, and all commuting and travelling activity ceased across the globe. Amongst all the other industries that were affected, one such was academia.

When the world went into lockdown in March 2020, education swiftly migrated online and people had to start teaching, learning, communicating and collaborating from their homes. Many universities lacked the experience and time they needed to conceive new ways to deliver instruction and assignments. Examinations were also affected, causing disruption to students' learning trajectories and progression. Student's expectations were altered and everyone entered into a world of the unknown. Across the sector, university management and academic staff had to change their focus from content to delivery. The main intentions were to be able to continue providing the same experiences online, as they would have done on campus. To be able to come up with a resolution to this urgent crisis wasn't easy and took a lot of time, effort, and iterations. The management and academic team at Regents University London successfully managed to devise a framework to incorporate the principals of academic delivery online. The main objectives behind the successful delivery and implementation of this framework were to facilitate engagement, provide ease of use, continuous support and through all this, a positive learning experience.

BACKGROUND MOTIVATION

The New Normal in Higher Education?

The shift to distance learning after the pandemic outbreak has happened suddenly and at a global scale. It was motivated and even forced by the existing situation (Cicha et al., 2021). The disruption caused to education by the pandemic has had a significant impact on the learning experience for students (Hill & Fitzgerald, 2020). Interactions and engagement have been impeded by the move to full online-delivery of teaching and learning (Hill & Fitzgerald, 2020). There were limited opportunities for synchronous discussion where all of the students would be online at the same time and the majority of engagement would need to occur through blog posts (Randsdell et. al, 2018).

Actively engaging students in learning is central to academic success and improved outcomes (Docherty et al., 2018). The use of online platforms such as Blackboard, can be useful to create discussion forums, provide feedback and participate in online discussions.

Before the pandemic outbreak, distance learning was broadly discussed, while in higher education, online teaching has been used for more than 20 years (Kerres, 2020; Küsel et al., 2020).

With online learning, it would be difficult to achieve this 'sense of belonging' as time spent with peers online would be limited, with some students being less engaged due to other commitments and as they try to juggle life. This lack of engagement during online learning between students and, between lecturers and students could be challenging (Bowcock & Peters, 2016). Numerous ways are noted in the literature to motivate and engage students including lecturer enthusiasm, interactive classes, engaging students through group activities and using effective teaching methods that promote active learning (Collaço, 2017; Race, 2007).

These conditions are difficult to maintain when teaching is restricted to online sessions. However, the recent shift in the teaching process has been forced by circumstances and forced both students and tutors to adapt to a new reality, despite the problems both of them have experienced. Furthermore, it was also an organizational challenge in terms of conducting the whole teaching process for universities worldwide. Researchers noted that many teachers quickly developed their digital competencies. Since the COVID-19 pandemic outbreak, studies have been conducted globally to analyse not only the universities' responses to the new situation (Crawford, 2020), but also its impact on students and their tutors. Analysis mostly focused on the quality of students' life during a pandemic (Aristovnik, 2020; (Wu et al., 2020), the process of online learning itself, and the impact of the pandemic on higher education institutions overall.

The impact of the pandemic has had far reaching implications overall for teaching and learning in Higher Education, where educators have reported that due to the immediate urgency of the lockdown there was little time to plan for online delivery and assessment (Garcia-Penalvo et al., 2020). In the short term, some institutions implemented immediate measures to support students and developed makeshift education systems to cope with the disruptions and impact of school and university closures.

Student Engagement and Expectation

Student experience can be reviewed with the help of four variables. They are;

- Engagement
- Perceived usefulness
- Perceived ease of use, and
- Support (Hill & Fitzgerald, 2020; Cicha et al., 2021).

And student engagement can often be indicated through association with their;

- Studies
- Tutors
- Peers (Zepke & Leach, 2010, 2014; Docherty et al., 2018).

Student engagement is a central concept in the literature on teaching and learning in higher education (Chapman, 2003). Higher engagement has been associated with a positive learning experience. Docherty et al., (2018) identified students' active engagement in learning as central to their academic success. Building relationships between students and lecturers can be beneficial for active engagement in classes (Dismore et al., 2019; Bramble et al., 2018). Reinke (2019) found that if students are emotionally engaged, they will experience emotive reactions including a sense of belonging, enjoyment, and interest, and when students feel this sense of belonging, their classroom engagement improves (Bryson, 2014). Marton and Saljo's seminal studies (1976a & 1976b) found that more deeply engaged students are motivated to learn by intrinsic interest in the subject rather than by fear of failing the assessments and that they are more likely to understand what they have learned. In a traditional academic setting, students have mostly had such engagement experiences in a physical setting.

However, such interactions and engagement have been impeded by the move to full online-delivery of teaching and learning (Hill & Fitzgerald,

2020). Engagement between students and lecturers was significantly hindered by moving workshops online, as the face-to-face time allowed relationships to be built with each of the lecturers (Hill & Fitzgerald, 2020.). As per a study conducted by (Bryson, 2014), when students are not engaged, this can be detrimental to their learning success and lead to feelings of disconnect. Furthermore, an absence of meaningful activities can lead to a more surface learning approach leading to poorer learning outcomes (Dolmans et al., 2016).

The other aspects that could affect student experience would be the perceived usefulness and perceived ease of use of distance learning (Cicha et al., 2021). In the context of distance learning, perceived usefulness is associated with the having the comfort of attending classes from their home. One of the things this has also given students is, an extended availability and access to their tutors. This would also then add to the extra help and support students would have had in completing their assessments.

Ease of use would be associated with the ability and willingness of students to use a virtual learning platform (Blackboard in the case of RUL). Since the lockdowns happened almost overnight, limited number of VLE platforms had the ability to provide a full engagement experience online (Adedoyin et al., 2020). However, these platforms were instantly updated to ensure that they could provide the environment to study and address demanding challenges and e-learning procedure factors during this epidemic. Students' ability to use their hardware and the various software to complete their class tasks or module assessments would also add to their learning experience. A key consideration when considering the student experience would be how far they felt supported throughout and if they got help when they needed it.

The RADAR Framework at Regents UNIVERSITY LONDON

In order to provide an excellent learning experience and hopefully improve their overall engagement, efforts and changes were made at pace to the learning and teaching strategy at Regents University London in the summer of 2020. In relation to this initiative, a learning design framework was proposed. The objective of this framework was to provide guidance to tutors, for the creation of the curriculum at both macro and micro levels. It offered a structure for thinking about learning outcomes, and an appropriate mix of activities that would enable students to meet those outcomes. The university required a new model of curriculum design to help them implement the new pedagogic principles that would also allow them to deliver a step-change in their approach to online learning. Specifically, there was a need to adopt a more active learning approach, by including challenge-based learning and collaboration while moving away from the traditional lecture/seminar format based on the transmission of content. There was a need for a new learning design framework that would work equally for online learning, due to restricted campus opening and/or social distancing requirements. The framework was required to help improve the student learning experience through greater structure in their learning and clarity about expected engagement. This is when the RADAR model was adopted. The acronym RADAR refers to five broad learning activities: Research, Acquire, Discuss, Action, Reflect.

RADAR helped create clear parameters for tutors to design and operationalise learning, while recognising **academics'** existing teaching and learning expertise, and reaffirming their ownership of the learning design process. The basis of this framework is rooted in tried and tested pedagogic research but offers sufficient flexibility to adapt effectively to all the different disciplines we offer. Furthermore, it builds structure, capacity and staff skills for the development of additional flexibly designed programmes in the future. The RADAR framework is detailed in table 1.

In conducting Research and Acquiring information, students are expected to learn through engaging with content, may it be academic, industry based, audio, visual or any other. The intention of this is to grow their knowledge and understanding around a particular topic. One of the aims of the R and A is also to teach students how to engage in academic research, and to be able to present their ideas and findings. The 'Discuss' phase is considered a very important step in a student's learning journey and somewhat challenging to facilitate in an online environment. However, through the implementation of the RADAR framework, a variety of options were created to provide students a platform and opportunities to engage with their peers and tutors. In keeping with the idea of providing experiential learning through the Action stage, students were taught how to use the knowledge gained from the previous phases to successfully attempt their assessments. Furthermore, the Reflection aspect allowed students and tutors to lookback on their experience, contributions and learning in order to improve future experiences. Thus, the RADAR framework was designed to provide students with an engaged, experiential and fulfilling online learning experience.

Table 1. The RADAR framework

	Learning Activities	Learning Type
RESEARCH	Learners use existing learning resources and/or find newones for their own intellectual enquiry and knowledge construction.	Experiential
ACQUIRE	Learning through listening, reading and watching (includingshort micro lectures from the tutor).	Didactic
DISCUSS	Learning through discussion and collaboration, with or without the tutor present, in small groups or large groups,structured or unstructured.	Collaborative
ACTION	Learners apply their understanding of the concepts toaddressing a challenge or producing an artefact or outcome (and receive tutor and/or peer feedback).	Experiential (& possibly collaborative)
REFLECT	Learners reflect on their experience and receive formativefeedback (including 1:1s).*	Experiential

(Regents University London, 2020)

Based on the work of Laurillard (2012) and Jennings (2013), learning types help us to focus on what learners are doing (as opposed to focusing on what teachers do). For a pedagogy based on active learning (rather than the transmission approach), and even more importantly, an online/distance learning environment, a typical weekly learning scheme for students needed to include a balance of experiential, collaborative and didactic learning elements, as close as possible to these proportions: Experiential = 70%, Collaborative = 20%, Didactic = 10%

This represents a clear move away from teacher-led activities such as lectures, hence the lower proportion of time dedicated to didactic learning.

Implementation of RADAR

In order to deliver an academic experience online, the most successful learning experiences were found to be based around flexible, well-paced design with clear learning outcomes in mind, that were mostly synchronous. Synchronous means discussion held in real-time, often using chat or messaging applications. Asynchronous discussion typically uses online discussion boards where students respond to comments and questions from class-members. The focus shifted from a traditional idea of total contact hours (what the teacher does), to total study or learning hours, where the student works through a set of carefully sequenced, rich and engaging learning activities. Discussion, engagement and collaboration with tutors and peers were deemed important, and was to be achieved through asynchronous as well as live activities.

The framework needed to balance the need for live discussion with the challenges that many students would face when required to access synchronous activities across different time zones, as well as recognising that active engagement could be better achieved by increasing experiential learning. To ensure that appropriate learning content would be accessible when delivered across several modules simultaneously, module developers needed to keep webinars to a shorter length, avoid overly long synchronous activities, reduce the number of live sessions each week (ideally one per week per module), and record any live presentation/lecture content. This was particularly so for many of the classes, which previously would have been delivered face-to-face and included interactive elements, where the content was uploaded to Blackboard (VLE) for students to read individually at their own pace.

The initial step of implanting the RADAR framework started by reviewing module learning outcomes. According to constructive alignment (Biggs and Tang, 2011), student learning outcomes (expressed as verbs indicating what learners need to be able to do) were needed to directly inform the learning activities designed for practice and engagement; these verbs would also be included in the allocated assessment tasks (Campbell & Mayer, 2009). Then, thinking about the learners' sequential and incremental development, tutors could assign weekly aims that break down the overall learning outcomes into more manageable units. These weekly aims would determine design of activities. Using the RADAR framework to design learning activities helped to provide a rich variety of content in easily digestible amounts, again, making sure that this would be suitable for delivery in the classroom or online. Careful structuring and sequencing of the activities also needed to allow students to navigate their weekly learning step-by-step, and at a reasonably flexible pace.

When designing assessment tasks, work started by checking that assessments would map against learning outcomes. Assessment briefs were tailored for completion and submission online. A focus on active learning meant increasing opportunities for students to engage with authentic assessments that would help incorporate real world tasks, projects and challenges - which could be both formative and summative. Senior et al., (2018) discovered that by giving students the opportunity to share their opinions, engagement levels improved. Live briefs or projects set by external industry guests, tasks that connect with how industry professionals in the field are responding to this new uncertain context, or activities such as quizzes that enable students to check their own progress and learning were also taken into consideration in developing the assessment tasks.

Wherever possible, students were to be given an opportunity to submit and get feedback on draft submissions which was seen to be a great way to support their learning, especially working remotely. The intention of the RADAR framework was set to provide continuous engagement, provide ease of use and access to materials, and improve perception of the learning experience online.

Outcomes of the Implementation of RADAR

A study was conducted to measure the outcome from implementation of the RADAR framework. In total, 28 masters level students participated in this study. Ten questions were asked based around the topics of; engagement, ease of use, perceived usefulness and support.

In the first question, students were asked to rate their experience of studying online and to that 35.71% (10) replied it as better than expected, and 46.43 (13) said it was as expected. 17.86% (5) said it didn't meet their expectations. The second question was about their engagement experience with their tutors and to that 78% (22) responded positively, 17.86% (5) responded as average and 3.57% (1) said it was poor. Question three asked about engagement with peers and to that, 67.86% (19) said it was positive, 14.29% (4) said it was average and 17.86% (5) said that their peer engagement was poor. Question 4 was related to the use of the VLE platform, and the outcome was that they 92.85% (26) felt confident engaging with the VLE platform for just 7.14% (2) said that they lacked the confidence. To the question about working on assessments online, 85.71% (24) students said that they were confident attempting and working through their online assessments and only 14.28% (4) mentioned that they lacked the confidence in this area. In terms of the support, they received throughout the online learning period, 53.57% (15) responded it was good, 42.86 (12) said it was satisfactory and only 3.57% (1) said it was poor. About a question related to perceived usefulness and on how they enjoyed the experience of working from home, only 21.43% (6) said it was good, 35.71% (10) said not so good and 42.86% (12) were unsure about it. A question on which kind of engagement was most useful in improving their online experience, 46.43% (13) rated engagement with tutors to be the highest. 25% (7) considered peer engagement to be the most important and 28.57% (8) reported engagement with the course through a VLE platform to be the most important to their online experience. Question 9 was assessing which factor to be the most important for their online experience and to that, extended access and engagement with tutors was rated highest 46.43% (13) followed by efficacy of working from home 35.17% (10) and lastly, the ease of use of the VLE platform at 17.86% (5). However, the last question was a great revelation. The last question was, which aspect of learning would be the most important in giving students a great learning experience, 75% (21) replied, on campus learning and 25% (7) mentioned the social aspect of being on campus which would relate to engagement. None of the students said that the online experience would come close to the one they would get in a traditional academic setting.

DISCUSSION AND CONCLUSION

The objective of the RADAR framework was to provide students, at a time of crisis, with a great learning experience through extended engagement and ease of usefulness. The RADAR framework was meant to give students a sense of belonging, a space to explore, learn and grow and most importantly create a great engaging experience. As can be seen from the outcome above, engagement seemed like the most important factor in improving student experience and within engagement, it was close engagement with tutors, peers and the VLE platform. Whilst Blackboard was a valuable learning platform, there were times where students found it may have impeded their learning. Despite academic staff creating an open and engaging environment, they felt they may have held back during discussions for fear of saying the wrong thing or being misjudged.

Blackboard Collaborate sessions were held with audio and video to facilitate students with an option of being able to 'see' their peers and lecturers and connect with them at a more personal level. This did facilitate group assessments and weekly tasks. When students talk about an extended access to tutors, this was facilitated by creating groups on MS Teams and WhatsApp. This provided an informal platform for student and tutor engagement, and one that the students appreciated. It may be noteworthy to mention, the potential of social networking platform such as WhatsApp in fostering connectedness within online student cohorts. Similar to the findings of Stone and Logan (2018) and Adedoyin (2020), the accessibility, convenience, speed, informalities and freedom to ask 'silly questions' was perceived favourably by students. WhatsApp had been referred to as a 'lifeline' where the interactions were described as being central to student engagement and completion of the course (Stone & Logan, 2018), which aligned with the experiences of students within this course.

Even for the question on working on assessments, engagement with tutors was seen to be important for students. Students reported higher engagement with meaningful activities that were linked to summative assessment and those activities with a personalised approach in which lecturers actively participated (Dyment et al., 2020; Randsdell et al., 2018). Responses on perceived usefulness were somewhat balanced between high for some to, low for some and yet unsure for a lot of them. However, the outcome from the final question was an eye opener. When asked, what would be the most important aspect to impact their education experience, the majority of the students responded by saying that it would be being on campus, and a fraction also going with the social engagement side of academia. This is in line with a statement by (Muhammad & Kainat, 2020) who suggest that the lack of face-to-face interaction with lecturers and other students has led to feelings of isolation, and is true for a lot of students taking their studies online. They further state that it could be challenging to continue to build these relationships with lack of contact, and therefore achieve full engagement within the online learning environment.

Whilst there was consistent learning material available via various virtual learning platforms for students to collaborate and remain interactive online, it is impossible to deny the feeling of isolation that COVID-19 exerted (Hill & Fitzgerald, 2020). From a student perspective, self-directed study time has increased (Aucejo et al., 2020), and so have the levels of stress and anxiety experienced by students (Karalis & Raikou, 2020; Baloran, 2020). During this period, there was a reduction in participation in some of the optional learning forums by most students due to the amount of time it took to ensure that entries in any online forum were reflecting academic writing standards with little direct benefit as marks were not awarded for participation.

Additionally, some students also missed connecting with peers face-to-face and learning informally from each other's experiences which always helped focus our learning whilst enhancing motivation to learn. This is in line with the responses of students in the survey. Some studies reported these activities as being of limited value to learning where student's participation was seen as "going through the motions' rather than actively engaging (Dyment et al., 2020). However, learning in a small group classroom provided a free, non-judgemental environment for students to explore, share ideas, create understandings, and find new meaning in their learning.

It can be concluded that, although the design and implementation of the RADAR framework would have succeeded in giving students an experiential, supportive and an engaged experience, it cannot be compared to the one gained through traditional on campus learning. Since the world is trying to get back to normality and places are opening up, there is hope that we will be able to go back to campus and enjoy the traditional learning experiences.

However, all the things that we have done and learned during the online phase should not go to waste. Some of the asynchronous activities could still be used to create a positive student engagement and more importantly, create a repository of information that could be used by future students throughout the term. Some of the elements of learning that might be lost in a traditional environment (for example: people sharing and contributing to ideas, all the sessions being recorded and available to access at any time), were actually captured relatively well in the online format. Instead of just focusing on the content; altering delivery methods and using a combination of synchronous and asynchronous methods will allow and facilitate extended learning for the students. This would provide them with opportunities to engage with their peers and tutors not just offline but also extend it online. Just as every cloud has a silver lining and every situation teaches us something, the COVID-19 pandemic has taught us that we can do anything when we work together even in adversity, and that there is always a solution to a problem.

REFERENCES

Adedoyin, O. B, Soykan, E. (2020). COVID-19 pandemic and online learning: The challenges and opportunities. *Interact. Learn. Environ*, 1–13.

Almaiah, M. A., Al-Khasawneh, A. & Althunibat, A (2020). Exploring the critical challenges and factors influencing the E-learning system usage during COVID-19 pandemic. *Educ. Inf. Technol. 25*, 5261–5280.

Aristovnik, A, Keržic, D, Ravšelj, D, Tomaževic, N, & Umek, L (2020). Impacts of the COVID-19 pandemic on life of higher education students: A global perspective. *Sustainability*. 12, 8438.

Bowcock, R., & Peters, K. (2016). Discussion Paper: Conceptual Comparison of Student and Therapeutic Engagement. *Nurse Education in Practice,* 17, 188-191.

Bryson, C. (2014). *Understanding and Developing Student Engagement.* Abingdon: Routledge.

Campbell, J., & Mayer, R. E. (2009). Questioning as an instructional method: Does it affect learning from lectures? *Applied Cognitive Psychology*, 23, (6), 747- 759.

Cicha, K, Rizun, M. Rutecka, P, & Strzelecki, A (2021). COVID-19 and Higher Education: First-Year Students' Expectations toward Distance Learning. *Sustainability*. 13, 1889. https://doi.org/10.3390/su1304 1889.

Collaço, C. M. (2017). Increasing student engagement in higher education. *Journal of Higher Education Theory and Practice,* 17, (4), 40-47.

Crawford, J, Butler-Henderson, K, Rudolph, J, Malkawi, B, Glowatz, M, Burton, R, Magni, P. A & Lam, S. (2020). COVID-19: 20 countries' higher education intra-period digital pedagogy responses. *J. Appl. Learn. Teach*. 2020, 3, 9–28.

Docherty, A., Warkentin, P., Borgen, J., Garthe, K. A., Fischer, K., & Najjar, R. (2018). Enhancing student engagement: innovative strategies for intentional learning. *Journal of Professional Nursing*, 34, (6), 470-474.

Dolmans, D., Loyens, S., Marcq, H., & Gijbels, D. (2016). Deep and surface learning in problembased learning: a review of the literature. *Advances in Health Sciences Education*, 21, (5), pp 1087–1112.

Dyment, J., Stone, C. & Milthorpe, N. (2020). Beyond busy work: rethinking the measurement of online student engagement. *Higher Education Research & Development*.

Hill, K. and Fitzgerald, R. (2020). Student perspectives of the impact of COVID-19 on learning. *All Ireland Journal of Higher Education*, 12(2).

Kerres, M. (2020). Against all odds: Education in Germany coping with COVID-19. *Postdigital Sci. Educ.* 22, 1–5.

Küsel, J, Martin, F, Markic, S. (2020). University students' readiness for using digital media and online learning—comparison between Germany and the USA. *Educ. Sci.* 10, 313.

Race, P. (2007). *The Lecturer's Toolkit: A Practical Guide to Assessment, Learning and Teaching*. London and New York: Routledge, Taylor and Francis Group.

Randsdell, S, Borror, J, & Su, H. (2018). Users not watchers: motivation and the use of discussion boards in online learning. *Distance Learning*, 15, (2), 35–39.

Sasson, I, Yehuda, I. and Malkinson, N. (2018). Fostering the skills of critical thinking and question-posing in a project-based learning environment. *Thinking Skills and Creativity*, 29, pp.203-212.

Senior, R. M, Bartholomew, P, Soor, A, Shepperd, Bartholomew, B, & Senior, C. (2018). The Rules of Engagement": Student engagement and motivation to improve the quality of undergraduate learning. *Frontiers in Education*, 3, (32).

Stone, S., & Loga, N. A. (2018). Exploring students' use of the social networking site WhatsApp to foster connectedness in the online learning experience. *Irish Journal of Technology Enhanced Learning*, 3, (1), 44-57.

Wu, S.-J, Chang, D.-F, Sun, F.-R (2020). Exploring college student's perspectives on global mobility during the COVID-19 pandemic recovery. *Educ. Sci.* 10, 218.

Zepke, N, & Leach, L. (2010) Improving student engagement: ten proposals for action. *Active Learning in Higher Education*, 11, (3), 167-177.

Zepke, N. Leach, L, & Butler, P. (2014). Student engagement: students' and teachers' perceptions. *Higher Education Research & Development*, 33, (2), 386-398.

In: The Impact of COVID-19 on Teaching ...   ISBN: 978-1-53619-947-5
Editors: S. Studente, S. Ellis et al.   © 2021 Nova Science Publishers, Inc.

Chapter 10

SUMMING UP THE IMPACT OF COVID-19 ON STUDENT EXPERIENCE AND EXPECTATIONS

Stephen Ellis, PhD

Regent's University London, London, United Kingdom

ABSTRACT

Amongst the many important questions that the public health crisis of 2020/21 has forced the higher education (HE) sector to confront is that of the student experience. This chapter brings together the themes from the previous chapters of this book and suggests at least some possible ways forward as the sector begins a recovery. The interest in student experience stems from the continued rise of commercialisation in university provision where the role of the student is more akin to that of consumers. However, the pandemic has added a nuance to this relationship as students have of necessity had to become more participative and actively involved in their studies so that the relationship is more of a partnership than consumer/producer.

The holistic package of the student experience has undoubtedly been radically shaken by COVID. The chapters in this book are testament to the way that some institutions have moved incredibly far and incredibly fast to

---

* Corresponding Author's E-mail: feelgood.ellis@gmail.com.

preserve what they feel is valued by their students. Only a detailed future evaluation will show if we focussed on the right things. The conclusion of this chapter sets out some effective steps forward as we see them.

Keywords: engagement, student expectations, commercialisation, social connectivity, learning community, chatbot

INTRODUCTION

As we emerge slowly from COVID, it is a time to re-evaluate what is now truly valued and expected by students and subsequently, how universities can best gear up to deliver to that expectation. Some may indeed be brave and bold and present a better, more viable alternative. We are very unlikely to witness a race back to restore very old and frankly outdated learning models.

Student experience monitoring has become a mini-industry in the sector with surveys, (both internal and external), an 'army' of programme representatives, University, Senate and Faculty committees, student union, QAA, added to a range of formal and informal complaints handling procedures are all ready to take a critical view on how students are experiencing their time at university. This 'army' is aimed at discovering and responding to 'issues' or problems, although in my experience, the fact that the same issues often recur regularly is clear testament to the lack of effectiveness of representation, or the responses, or both.

Survey based data has many recognised imperfections, so gauging the true quality of the student experience is still sometimes unclear. They are often based on perceptions where the student has very limited experience of what an excellent experience would look like. Indeed, the very concept of an excellent experience may well differ widely between those answering the questions. This is not like a traditional consumer comparing product 'A' with products 'B,' C and 'D,' which might be a relatively easily comparison. Secondly, the surveys are usually restricted to captive participants already in the system, not those who did not enter, or did but have subsequently departed for whatever reason. So very valuable feedback is instantly lost.

Further, student evaluation surveys are almost always long after the event, generating very low participation (typically under 20%), as students see little or no value to them in participating.

One consequence of the COVID crisis has been to shine a very bright light on this area where there may well be significant gaps and, some would argue, a fundamental discrepancy between what institutions see as most valuable to the student experience and what the students themselves do. This book has detailed a number of responses where a delicate balance has been achieved in a true crisis situation between what the delivering institution sought to achieve and what their students wanted and could cope with.

This chapter concludes with some suggested steps to take the student experience/expectation question forward, beyond crisis management but fully embracing the learning of the past few months.

METHOD

This chapter was constructed in two ways. Firstly, a review of the content of the previous chapters to discern a series of key themes and foci and secondly, new evidence was obtained from individually conducted semi-structured interviews with 5 first year undergraduates from a range of institutions in the UK during the month of March 2021, after all had been the recipients of a COVID impacted year.

The wholly qualitative responses from the participants were subsequently summarised to complement the issues raised elsewhere in this book, but from a purely recipient perspective. The participants and their institutions were granted anonymity to ensure that their responses were both open and frank.

CHANGING STUDENT EXPECTATIONS

2020 saw an unprecedented challenge for all those in the university sector which has for hundreds of years been at the centre of broader societal development. Willets (2017), calls them the institutional equivalent of the California redwood trees. They are in many cases deep rooted, long lived and have significant power to shape the ecosystem around them. Perhaps this longevity has spawned some overconfidence? With 500 years of growth and expansion (UNESCOs HE World Database now lists over 10,000 institutions with the word 'University' in their title), why should a mere pandemic deflect them? To their credit the vast majority proved to be far more flexible than we might have imagined developing new, creative and innovative approaches to the challenge virtually overnight.

In the UK University, student retention rates are typically reported around the 70-75% mark, meaning that many students drop out before completing their studies for whatever reason. Expectations not being met are surely one of the causes of drop out and many institutions have increased their attention to this area through resourcing greater student support, for example by making counselling and mental health interventions more widely accessible. Demand for student support services however is rising to help meet ever increasing student expectations, but the picture could get much worse as worrying concerns over student wellbeing and inclusivity are now becoming heard ever more loudly. The changes imposed so swiftly by the pandemic has opened up the debate again around commercialisation, but the rise of technology supported learning, internet-based repositories of knowledge has also fundamentally shifted the 'producer power' advantage of even the most ancient and respected universities.

As the internet can now deliver instantly, 24/7 validated, answers for the majority of all undergraduate student queries around established knowledge and its application, the value of attending a university education cannot be hung merely on knowledge acquisition. Skills based programmes can also be hugely supported if not replaced by 'You-Tube' tutorials on pretty much any subject with video practical examples for students to emulate. So the role of the historic, traditional university as the sole guardian and disseminator of skills and knowledge is really no more. The internet as we know has now become the world's free library 'open all hours.' The other key university role of creating new knowledge through research undoubtedly remains significant but so does the question of who can and should finance this function? There is a clear tension between academic staff seeking to work on the sexy end of knowledge creation, vital to any university mission and the less exciting for many, demands of teaching and assessing students. As a Dean I was extremely aware of this tension as my colleagues often sought to focus their workloads away from what some saw as the chore of teaching and on to the pleasure of their personal research agenda, often with scant regard as to where the funding for such activity was secured.

Seldon (2018) outlines a number of seemingly intractable problems with conventional approaches to education even before the COVID crisis. These range from an inability to defeat deeply entrenched social immobility (despite numerous attempts to address this at the highest level), through inflexibility of progression, (the typical three-year UK undergraduate programme has remained largely unchanged despite the speed with which the very techniques that knowledge and learning is acquired have advanced). Seldon (2018) also adds in an overwhelming burden of administration, larger than ever class sizes, (commercialisation again), and homogenisation as restrictive factors propping up the existing, wholly inadequate traditional factory-based system.

Students have historically travelled quite willingly to where the knowledge or experience they seek is located in order to absorb it. But with knowledge widely available everywhere and the changes to online delivery forced through by the pandemic the knowledge location factor, driving residential based university programmes has been severely questioned. There will therefore need to be other compelling reasons for students to incur the cost and disruption of relocating, to enjoy and live the 'university experience' if the student halls are to remain occupied. Campuses clearly need students to thrive or even exist. The revenue from non-academic but vital residential, catering and associated fees remains crucial to the budgets of most universities. COVID removed much of this aspect of university life, which is impossible to move well to an online world, within weeks. Agreed budgets and plans were suddenly irrelevant as I found in my role as Dean. On top of which the additional costs and time required in reshaping the curriculum to online delivery mode were added.

Whether this is merely a temporary hit that will right itself as COVID ends or a fundamental reverse, we will need to judge in the future. But assets like large university buildings, and other resources designed precisely to be populated by hundreds of people, are not easy, cheap, or quick to convert to new purposes. They will sit 'sulking' on the balance sheets of the institution needing to be maintained, cleaned and insured, etc. for some time yet.

Interviews conducted for this book with first year undergraduate students who have experienced a COVID restricted year provided some interesting and challenging data. The questions asked included:

- What are your expectations of a university, how far were they met?
- What were the top 5 things that were significant in your decision to go to university?
- What looking back would you change about your experience?
- Was your experience good value for your time and money?
- What alternatives to going to university if any did you consider?

In response to the first question the opportunity to meet a diversity of people and make new friends was very much in the thoughts of those students interviewed. Although this was adjusted understandably in the light of the COVID situation, it is reasonable to assume that this need for developing personal networks, fuelled by close personal contact will not disappear. Outside of the academic environment the provision of societies, social events, political groups, hobbies, sports, etc. all make up the experience and the pandemic has largely reduced these to minimal proportions and in many cases have been totally closed down. However, this expectation remains a strong driver of what a strong university experience should be according to our respondents.

Interviewees further responded that their (UK) universities were slow to act in Sept/Oct 2020 when the likely impact of COVID was still to be confirmed. Typically, they opened up with restrictions in place and quickly invented ways of muddling through, such as intermittent seminars versus online tutoring. Virtual fresher's fairs were hastily prepared and attempts to relieve student anxiety were put in place. But as it quickly became clear that universities were becoming 'super spreaders' by gathering together people often into small spaces from all around the country and beyond, infection rates soared, with no vaccine yet available, students quickly began to opt out of any activities that were still functioning through understandable fear.

In terms of the student experience universities were unable to recreate on campus life and many students fed back that they had to quickly adjust their expectations in the hope that the situation would quickly return to normal once the disease was controlled.

One student reported that she arrived at her university with the expectation that the three years of her degree was going to be 'the best years of her life' having achieved the grades required to attend her choice of institution, so for her to say that the experience was a major let down is obviously understandable. Leaving home and committing to a new and often challenging social and intellectual environment is a tough ask in the best of times, especially for students who have not previously been independent. Adding to this usual level of anxiety, being widely exposed to a new and highly infectious and debilitating disease was obviously an additional worry, for students and their parents, hardly conducive to a positive experience for any provider.

Interviewees did also highlight that their universities had not acted well in regard to the costs they had to bear particularly around accommodation. Hall rooms were paid for up front even though there was a reasonable expectation that they would not be usable once the pandemic took hold. Indicating that students are increasingly expecting universities to provide value for money. Although a few universities have subsequently compensated accommodation fees in part, one interviewee reported that students were told that only those with no belongings in their rooms could get refunded, but they were not allowed to go on site to retrieve them! This is surely an action that smacks of putting the interest of a severely pressured balance sheet above that of students.

When asked more generally, what the top things that were significant about going to university were, 'meeting new people,' 'learning more about the subject area' and 'becoming more employable' consistently scored highly. Becoming more independent' was also seen as a key factor.

Achieving significant progress in these areas under COVID conditions has been incredibly tough and it is unlikely that this would be very effective without significant changes in practice and a redeployment of resources. Being aware that these are the chief factors that students value most highly is a great stimulus to the priorities of the build back and suggests that a wholly online experience is not going to fully replace the campus life style very soon.

Interestingly the interviewees were relatively satisfied with the academic provision under lockdown as their institutions rapidly shifted delivery to exclusively online or a blend of modes. Some reported that the tuition time had not really been impacted that much, although some did feel that they would have had more access to tutors under normal conditions. There was also a strong feeling that the perceived reduced costs of delivery online should have been passed on to the students to provide more value for money in some way. They felt strongly that they were paying the standard fees for the delivery of a very non-standard and in their eyes less satisfactory model.

It would appear from the responses that universities have generally not done a good job in communicating the reality that online provision is not that much cheaper than on campus once the costs of preparation, delivery technology, etc. are factored in, and the existing fixed costs of premises as already mentioned remain.

Interviewees also reported that they were aware from friends and students at other universities that some institutions had significantly reduced contact and that they felt fortunate that their programmes were relatively unaffected indicating a mix of responses from different institutions, not all positive. In terms of student expectation, this is a strong indication that students can and will evaluate their experience relative to their peers and friends elsewhere although this crucial aspect is rarely captured in current survey work.

When asked about their best and worst experiences of the year, responses highlighted the positive manner that small group online breakouts were able to foster more social interaction. This is in spite of the fact that most respondents reported that both they and their fellow students in such arenas were very reluctant to turn their cameras on! On the downside the way that their respective universities handled the transition from normality through blended to off campus was for some highlighted as poor, unsettling, badly communicated and in some cases divisive.

Interviewees were finally asked to consider what they would say after their recent experiences to someone considering going to university in September (2021). Given the impact of COVID one might expect this to be a mixed response, but the overwhelming reaction was still largely positive to the overall university experience but with one strong caveat. Being clear and sure about your reasons for going to university was said to be vital. Just going to university 'for the sake of it' without a clear purpose and forethought was seen as being too much of an expensive risk.

The potential impact of the course on your future career aspirations was thought to be a very significant factor in the decision, demonstrating that students expect this to be a vital factor in their overall experience. If the responses above are found to be typical then one impact of COVID may have been to sharpen the focus of what university education is for and about.

HAS COVID CHANGED OUR UNDERSTANDING OF WHAT A UNIVERSITY IS FOR?

This is a massive question and not one for this book to consider in depth but for Willets (2017), there is an all-pervasive advantage to society of university education, therefore the more people who go, the better both for themselves and for the wider world. For economic, social and societal developmental grounds, university attendees all tend to significantly outperform non attendees, although he admits there may be some inherent, self-selection bias here. Seldon (2018) looks more to the future in a discussion of how Artificial Intelligence (AI) will have increasing influence over the education world arguing that the future of university education will diverge into one of 6 varieties:

Table 1. Future Universities and expectations

Future type of University (Sheldon 2018)	Expectations addressed	Comment
Global	Leading post graduate researchers, reduced teaching, elite, tackling global problems internationally co-operative, highly influential at a policy level	How will this be funded? Essentially a research institution not focussed on teaching. Elite focus will severely restrict numbers and highly specialised commercially viable research will crowd out other areas. Very attractive for academic staff.
National	Predominantly for students seeking an on-campus experience. Teaching to the fore but some high level research being conducted.	Again seems to be a creation for the benefit of the academic staff rather than considering what on campus students will actually want or expect.
Regional	More focussed on home based students, very limited scope for research.	Basically an FE college as exists now but with degree awarding powers or aspirations.
Professional	Training specific to the needs of employers as required by the various professions.	Currently these exist as hybrid or offshoots from existing universities therefore ensuring the QA process.
Digital	No physical presence required. Ideal for students seeking total flexibility and not concerned about the social on site experience.	Will need to compete with blended offers increasingly being devised by existing institutions
Local	Technical, vocational and applied undergraduate studies. Mostly part time students.	Not what is currently considered to be the function of a university

The table on the previous page lays out some options briefly, but they all reflect a very producer orientated approach, not one which puts student expectations at the centre. The technological advances that we have seen over the last year, added to changes in pedagogic approach, has undoubtedly created to opportunity for more diversity, but it seems to be driven more by what we can do, not what we should. How do we know if students will warm to any of these models, or will the technological advances be enough to provide the drive?

CONCLUSION

Technology

The first section of this book focussed on the impacts of technology in the responses to the pandemic. Clearly some of these responses were likely to happen irrespective of the COVID stimulus but they have undoubtedly been hastened in their gestation. The transition to online pedagogy models was only possible because of the technology platforms available and academics with little or no knowledge of their operation had to run fast to catch the wave of the new models. Students also had to accept the new reality of online learning, 'knowledge based working' (Ellis 2006) and this was not always an easy fix.

There were numerous challenges in bringing technological solutions to bear, not least of which was the lack of resources to achieve their required rapid deployment. In addition, the move to online delivery had to be fully cognisant of the dangers of increased isolation, lack of interaction, which is a key driver of learning, and both staff and student wellbeing.

We saw that the online world brought with it the clear danger of students 'hiding' and their progression being harder to monitor support and develop by tutors if they chose to be less engaged with their studies. The concept of inclusive active distant learning is a guard against isolation to some degree. It also reflects the moves already made by some institutions to remove the lecture mode of tuition in favour of more impactful pedagogic models. The digitally rich environment so created holds out much hope for those in favour of moving further to an online world for the future of education provision. The use of simulations, AI, and virtual reality may well provide a greatly enriched learning environment for those with the resources and approach to support this mode of learning.

The development of chatbots in the education sphere also offers great hope in bridging the isolation gap that some fear will hold students back if they are not able to engage fully on campus. However, experience of very variable student attendance to academic events pre-pandemic is not one that supports the view that campus provision is the only or best solution.

Chatbots are increasingly enhancing transactions in many other commercial areas, so why would education seek to be excluded? The use of chatbots to build and drive self-sustaining learning communities is still a largely unexplored field and one that provides much potential.

This section also details a view that 'one size fits all' is not an acceptable approach to the delivery of the undeniable benefits of a university education. The transitions enabled and facilitated by universities are often complex and varied depending so much on the starting point of the individual. Some students arrive at their course with much more experience and confidence than their peers, and the job of the university is surely to support all levels as they require it. Simple logistical changes to the learning journey like having elements of orientation and elements of exit or 'wrapping up' to every module are significant steps towards recognising the individuality not conformity that technology can support.

Education and Wellbeing

The condition of student wellbeing has been a growing concern in recent years. Many students are reporting increased anxiety, feelings of isolation and mental health challenges at a time when they should be enjoying and developing their confidence to meet the challenges of the future. This section provides clear evidence that the COVID crisis has diverted more attention to this area which can be seen as a positive development brought about by the pandemic.

The earliest incarnation of online mass participation in learning, MOOCS, have been seen to be less successful in achieving completion partly due to the lack of tailoring to individual need and low levels of peer support. The chapter provides clear guidance that the best results, from a learning perspective, are achieved when we can create effective and strong alignment of the tutor, the learning materials and crucially the learner. That means that all three have to play their part in the tailoring process.

It also means that much thought and resourcing has to go into the preparation of learning to facilitate conditions that allow for this alignment.

Considering the arriving student individually, what their needs, hopes, fears and aspirations are would be a great benefit to enhance engagement before the programme of learning even commences. Technology can help here as more detailed profiles of all students can be easily obtained.

Engagement, Experience and Expectations

The final section of the book invites the reader to widen their perspectives on student engagement. Arguing that much more personalisation through self-reflection within the curriculum can be a driver of engagement itself. As we seek to identify and cater for the 'ideal learner' we must remember that they probably **don't** exist and all learners will have their own strengths *and* weaknesses, which is why they are learners, and need to be supported.

We can use the data from more sophisticated learner analytics which will give us more and more data on behaviours, actions and some data on preferences, and may point us in a range of directions. However, we must not forget that each learner is unique and probably less confident than we think. Learner analytics can give us largely quantitative data but is not very strong on the qualitative side. We can know for example precisely how often a student has visited a VLE site, but that does not give us any indication of the quality of the interactions and the learning they have achieved. Inferring engagement purely from the analytics is a dangerous route the tutor will still need to continue to be the judge and effective supporter in this matter.

We saw also in this section that when asked about the future of their education provision there was a strong desire to return to a campus-based model. The students who were surveyed were largely very appreciative of the efforts made to preserve their provision, but were equally convinced that it was not what they were expecting, or feel entitled to. Social engagement was seen as a crucial factor in their development and progression, and this should be no surprise to those with experience in the area. We must be sure that in our rush to preserve what we thought was most important, the academic experience, we have not lost sight of the non-academic experiences that are so vital to the holistic education provided by a university.

Future Steps and Recommendations

Combining the evidence presented from the proceeding chapters there are some clear, positive steps that we believe will move the sector forward to a post pandemic improvement in provision. These are outlined here;

- Seek to enhance the individualised support for students, driven through the application of enhanced technology to closely identify needs preferably pre arrival, to foster a much greater tailoring of provision.
- Help students to adjust to the new normal delivery model through 'learning how to learn' orientation to include managing and maximising the benefit form your engagement with online learning (- e.g., developing the confidence to turn your camera on!)
- Foster the growing benefits of peer support - ensure that students see and feel the benefit of being truly supported and of being a true supporter via the curriculum.
- Promote the strong development of a 'learning community' as the overarching ambition of the university. One that will sustain it through adversity, clarify its purpose and be a rallying call for all.

It is clear from the evidence in this book that the expectations of HE students in the light of COVID have been revised. It could also be argued that this is part of a natural evolution of expectations that can be seen in many markets, (although very much speeded up). The products and services I choose to buy now are unlikely to be the same as they were 10 years ago. The relationship between producer and consumer is ever evolving and what was satisfactory before is often inadequate when a new rival product or service changes the game and if we wish our students to be true consumers then they must have an effective voice to play that role.

When I first left my academic working life back in 1999, I spent 11 years in a financial services commercial environment. Upon my return to academia, I was amazed to find that virtually nothing had changed. Maybe I was just unlucky, but I found that the programmes, most of the content, assessment techniques, and delivery models were virtually identical. I can think of no other sector business or otherwise, where such stagnation would be possible. COVID has propelled rapid change in all HE institutions, but in many ways it is really a catching up rather than pioneering type of change.

In truth some of the new practices outlined in this book are merely adjusting rapidly to the way technology has evolved over time and universities have for whatever reason, (complacency?), ignored. The changes reported here have been mostly driven very effectively by individuals or small delivery teams at the coalface, not generally from director level, (although they will undoubtedly have supported them), demonstrating the wealth of talent that is around in many of our universities.

Many universities are or at least see themselves as 'anchor institutions' providing a backcloth for their local economies. An anchor institution, as the name implies, is one that others can both relate to and rely on as a beacon through tough times. They are also major employers in their locality, both directly and indirectly. They also provide talent, advice and often the physical premises for local businesses and interest groups to integrate with their community and beyond. But the impact of the pandemic has served to at least temporarily untether these anchors. Universities perhaps thought and behaved as though they would be around, largely unchanged forever, and now have to seriously consider their own future place and role in their communities and most importantly how to meet their clients evolving expectations.

> 'Our institutions, corporations and organisations need to reform to be prepared, to maintain trust and stay relevant. This requires the development of a mind-set prepared constantly to review their relationship with the society they serve, and with the ecosystems in which they operate and influence' Heffernan (2020).

Like other employers in pandemic crisis, universities have furloughed staff, restricted public access due to safety issues, and curtailed much of the activity that their communities were once openly welcomed to. These bridges will need to be reviewed and rebuilt, or other bridges formed.

Change often derives energy from people's dissatisfaction. There is evidence that students don't consistently get that which they expected from their universities, now we have an amazing opportunity to respond positively to the challenges of meeting revised student expectations. Using the pandemic as a reason, and a legitimate excuse to re-orientate around what students really want and increasingly expect to get can only be a good thing and confirm that universities are not just for today but also for unborn future generations. The pandemic may prove to give a voice to those who were previously largely unheard. Students might well be one of these groups and they will become more, not less vocal. Most universities have a student experience strategy, but it is hard to see how this can be an offshoot, or accompaniment to any other strategy. Surely improving and maintaining an excellent and consistent student experience is THE only strategy? Commercialism means customer/students getting more of what they want and pay for, and less of what they don't want. As a demanding customer they expect to be treated well, listened to, understood and even sometimes delighted with their experience.

REFERENCES

Ellis, S. (2006) *Knowledge Based Working*. Chandos Publishing.

Heffernan, M. (2020) *Unchartered*. Simon and Schuster.

Seldon. A. (2018) *The Fourth Education Revolution*. University of Buckingham Press.

Willets, D. (2017) *A University Education*. Oxford University Press.

ABOUT THE EDITORS

Sylvie Studente is an Assistant Professor at Regent's University London. With over 20 years research experience, she has led, and contributed to a number of international research projects. Sylvie obtained her PhD in Human Computer Interaction in 2008 from the Knowledge Media Institute at The Open University, and has since completed a number of additional post-graduate studies in Education. Her BA and MSc are in the areas of Business and Computing. Her research interests span the areas of; education, assessment, e-learning, and technology. Prior to her position at Regent's University, she taught at a number of other HE institutions leading courses on; Interaction Design, Artificial Intelligence, Marketing and Project Management. Sylvie also has industry experience in the fields of; Project Management, Artificial Intelligence and Interaction Design in both business and education contexts. As well as her duties at Regent's University London, Sylvie is an External Examiner for Digital Business at the University of Westminster, and a Doctoral Supervisor for the University of Northampton. She is a member of the Advisory Board for the Journal of Knowledge Management, Economics and Information Technology, and a member of the editorial board for the Journal of Psychological Research.

Stephen Ellis holds both PFHEA and Chartered Manager accreditation, reflecting his twin track career in management and educator. He joined Regents University in 2014 after 4 years at University of Chichester. He returned to academia following 11 years with HSBC as an international management development specialist, and latterly as a senior HR business partner. He previously worked in a range of educational roles for over 20 years. He completed his PHD on Knowledge Management with the University of Bradford in 2006 which was subsequently published as a textbook on Knowledge Based Working. He obtained his first degree from Manchester University, a PhD from Bradford University and an MBA from Henley and has published books on Organisational Behaviour, Knowledge Management and Flexible working. Steve has worked in 10 culturally diverse countries and has managed significant HR change and development projects in the financial services industry. His current research interests focus on using chatbot potential to engage students. In the past he has consulted on organisational performance and employee engagement.

Originally from Sheffield, he now lives in Surrey and his outside interests include music (playing and listening) and supporting the not so mighty 'Blades'.

Bhavini Desai is an Associate Professor and Director of Content for areas of; Brand Management and Marketing at Regents University London. With over 15 years of academic experience in Digital Marketing & Data Analytics, Bhavini has balanced this with industry experience from consultancy work in private and public sectors. From 2002-2006, she worked at Brunel University as a Researcher on an Economic and Social Research Council project funded by the Engineering and Physical Sciences Research Council (EPSRC). In her role as a Head of Programme, Bhavini had been responsible for Monitoring and improving the development and delivery of modules on the programme, Enhancement of Student Experience, Engagement with and improvement of Student Recruitment and Retention, Liaison with relevant internal and external constituents and has successfully led the programme through a revalidation. Her research interests lie in the areas of innovation and adoption of emerging technologies for digital marketing with a particular interest in Changes in consumer behaviour, Marketing to the New Age Digital Customers, Big Data Management and Strategic Management. She has published articles in journals, conferences and books as well as coedited them. Bhavini is currently acting as a reviewer for a journal and a SIG chair.

INDEX

A

academic performance, xii, 97, 98, 99, 102, 103

academic success, xii, 111, 112, 115, 161, 177, 179

acculturation, 97, 102, 110

adjustment, 31, 55, 73

alcohol use, 106

anchor institutions, 207

anxiety, viii, xii, xv, 15, 52, 56, 67, 72, 95, 96, 97, 98, 99, 100, 101, 105, 106, 107, 110, 161, 187, 198, 199, 204

anxiety disorder, 95, 96

artificial intelligence, 53, 135

assessment, viii, xiii, xiv, xv, 56, 65, 67, 85, 86, 100, 176, 178, 184, 187, 207, 209

assessment techniques, 207

asynchronous activities, 188

attendance, xiii, 83, 151, 152, 153, 155, 156, 158, 159, 160, 162, 163, 166, 168, 171, 203

autonomy, 23, 37, 40, 43, 162, 165

B

balance sheet, 198, 199

barriers, xiii, 47, 92, 102, 152, 156, 160, 161, 170

behaviour change, xi, 77, 79, 84, 85, 86, 117, 125, 126, 127, 128, 130

beneficial effect, 5

benefits, x, xiii, 34, 52, 53, 56, 58, 68, 103, 128, 129, 163, 167, 204, 206

C

capacity building, 2, 8, 11, 13, 16, 18

career development, 73

challenges, viii, ix, xii, xv, 3, 4, 5, 7, 11, 12, 14, 17, 18, 27, 40, 43, 53, 54, 56, 59, 68, 69, 75, 79, 82, 83, 108, 109, 112, 113, 119, 131, 135, 161, 162, 170, 180, 183, 184, 189, 203, 204, 208

chatbot, v, x, 51, 52, 53, 54, 55, 56, 57, 58, 60, 61, 62, 63, 65, 67, 69, 71, 72, 73, 194, 210

childhood, 140

children, 38, 39, 88, 107, 136

civil service, 139, 144, 145

clarity, 154, 181
classes, 3, 4, 6, 7, 10, 12, 13, 16, 17, 18, 55, 63, 80, 82, 83, 87, 139, 143, 178, 179, 180, 183
classroom, vii, viii, 1, 2, 4, 6, 8, 11, 15, 16, 20, 42, 80, 82, 92, 159, 168, 179, 184, 188
classroom activity, 11
classroom settings, viii
clients, xii, 112, 122, 123, 207
closure, vii, x, xi, 68, 96, 97, 98, 100, 102
cognitive process, 26
cognitive processing, 26
cognitive psychology, 138
cognitive style, 91
collaboration, xiii, 16, 18, 24, 31, 34, 35, 38, 40, 41, 82, 151, 155, 181, 182, 183
colleges, 32, 134, 172
commercial, 134, 138, 141, 204, 207
commercialisation, 193, 194, 196, 197
communication, 26, 36, 52, 61, 62, 72, 87, 117, 140, 147
compassion, 121, 122, 123, 124, 125
compassion fatigue, 120, 121, 122, 123, 124, 125
connectivity, 53, 59, 62, 194
construction, 23, 24, 27, 36, 43, 147, 173, 182
constructive alignment, 80, 90, 93, 183
coping strategies, xv, 73, 108, 117
correlation analysis, 59
cost, 120, 121, 130, 135, 156, 166, 197
course content, 11, 40, 126, 128, 131
COVID-19, v, vi, vii, viii, ix, x, xii, xiii, xv, xvi, 1, 2, 19, 20, 39, 41, 51, 55, 68, 69, 70, 71, 72, 73, 74, 77, 78, 80, 81, 82, 92, 93, 96, 100, 105, 106, 107, 108, 109, 110, 111, 112, 120, 121, 125, 127, 130, 131, 151, 152, 160, 161, 162, 165, 169, 173, 175, 176, 178, 187, 188, 189, 190, 193

creative process, 25
creative thinking, 45
crisis management, 195
critical thinking, 36, 38, 190
cross sectional study, 108
cross-sectional study, 105, 107, 110
curriculum, 92, 110, 143, 144, 145, 146, 167, 181, 197, 205, 206

D

Department of Health and Human Services, 21
depression, xii, 56, 95, 96, 97, 98, 99, 100, 101, 105, 106, 107, 110
depth, 35, 38, 88, 141, 149, 173, 201
distance education, 45, 102
distance learning, 30, 47, 101, 102, 135, 177, 178, 180, 182
diversity, 23, 29, 30, 42, 43, 44, 90, 91, 152, 154, 161, 171, 198, 202

E

eBooks, 88
ecosystem, 196
education, vii, viii, x, xi, xii, xiii, xiv, xv, 2, 3, 4, 6, 13, 18, 19, 24, 28, 42, 45, 47, 56, 57, 68, 69, 71, 74, 77, 78, 79, 85, 90, 91, 92, 96, 102, 106, 108, 110, 111, 112, 113, 115, 116, 119, 120, 125, 131, 132, 135, 136, 137, 142, 144, 145, 147, 148, 149, 169, 175, 176, 177, 178, 187, 197, 201, 203, 205, 209
education principles, 78
educational experience, 3, 86, 90, 134
educational opportunities, 28
educators, viii, ix, xiii, 2, 3, 4, 5, 6, 7, 8, 9, 10, 11, 12, 13, 14, 15, 16, 17, 30, 39, 43, 45, 55, 57, 77, 79, 91, 133, 135, 138, 143, 147, 173, 178

e-learning, x, 20, 68, 180, 209
emergency, 5, 73, 74, 121, 122, 162
emotional experience, 34
emotional intelligence, 109
engagement, viii, ix, x, xi, xiii, xiv, 24, 25, 26, 27, 28, 30, 32, 34, 35, 37, 38, 39, 40, 43, 48, 52, 54, 58, 59, 61, 64, 65, 67, 79, 85, 98, 99, 104, 107, 109, 128, 131, 132, 143, 151, 152, 153, 154, 155, 156, 157, 158, 159, 160, 161, 162, 163, 164, 167, 168, 170, 171, 172, 173, 175, 176, 177, 178, 179, 180, 183, 184, 185, 186, 187, 189, 190, 194, 205, 206, 210, 211
environment, 2, 3, 4, 5, 8, 11, 15, 16, 26, 27, 28, 29, 30, 39, 40, 42, 44, 46, 53, 54, 57, 78, 88, 94, 97, 102, 103, 130, 138, 144, 153, 160, 180, 181, 182, 186, 187, 188, 198, 199, 203, 207
epidemic, 106, 107, 110, 180
evidence, 61, 85, 105, 120, 127, 138, 146, 152, 157, 159, 163, 168, 195, 204, 206, 208
expertise, 14, 79, 89, 181

F

face-to-face interaction, viii, x, 52, 67, 147, 187
fear, 137, 141, 179, 186, 199, 203
feelings, viii, x, 51, 52, 54, 55, 63, 67, 68, 87, 97, 99, 101, 102, 161, 180, 187, 204
flexibility, 40, 42, 82, 87, 91, 98, 161, 165, 167, 181, 202
flipped classroom approach, 80
focus groups, 52, 58, 60, 61, 155
formation, 47, 49, 127, 130
free online short courses, 113

G

gender differences, 109

general practitioner, 122
global mobility, 190
global scale, 82, 177
graduate students, 58, 63, 100
guidance, 6, 48, 105, 138, 139, 160, 181, 204

H

health, xii, 5, 40, 42, 77, 97, 99, 103, 104, 106, 107, 108, 109, 112, 113, 115, 119, 120, 121, 122, 124, 125, 126, 131, 160
health care, 113, 120, 122
health care professionals, 113, 120
health status, 106
high school, 109
higher education, viii, xiii, xiv, xv, xvi, 2, 5, 22, 30, 32, 41, 45, 46, 48, 51, 52, 54, 57, 67, 68, 69, 70, 71, 72, 73, 74, 75, 77, 78, 92, 93, 96, 106, 109, 132, 134, 135, 147, 148, 154, 165, 167, 168, 169, 170, 171, 172, 173, 175, 176, 177, 178, 179, 189, 190, 191, 193
history, 73, 105, 150
human, 3, 5, 79, 146, 172, 176

I

inclusion, 9, 28, 29, 30, 32, 42, 44, 48, 113, 152, 156, 161, 167, 168, 170, 172
individual students, 83, 97, 105, 154, 164, 167
individuals, 41, 105, 138, 158, 207
industry, 77, 80, 181, 184, 194, 209, 210, 211
institutions, vii, viii, xiii, xiv, 2, 54, 175, 178, 193, 195, 196, 200, 202, 203, 207, 209
instructor presence, 87, 91

Index

isolation, viii, x, xii, 52, 54, 55, 63, 67, 68, 70, 73, 87, 91, 99, 100, 101, 102, 112, 160, 187, 203, 204

K

kindergarten children, 47
knowledge acquisition, 83, 196
knowledge based working, 203, 208, 210

L

lack of confidence, 7
lack of opportunities, 97
landscape, vii, xiv, 51, 53
leadership, 18, 49, 146
learner analytics, 152, 205
learners, ix, xi, 11, 23, 25, 26, 27, 29, 30, 31, 32, 34, 38, 40, 41, 43, 79, 85, 86, 87, 88, 89, 90, 91, 97, 104, 127, 133, 134, 138, 139, 141, 142, 143, 145, 146, 147, 157, 182, 184, 205
learning activity, 37, 117
learning community, 20, 27, 44, 64, 65, 194, 206
learning environment, ix, 24, 26, 29, 30, 43, 46, 72, 88, 92, 93, 115, 131, 139, 142, 190, 203
learning outcomes, 23, 43, 47, 143, 163, 165, 180, 181, 183, 184
learning process, 27, 29, 35, 68, 98
learning skills, 34
learning styles, 138
learning task, 64
lesson plan, 9, 10, 42
level of education, 59
life experiences, 161
lifelong learning, 41
loneliness, 54, 55, 68, 70, 74, 99, 100, 102

M

majority, xi, 3, 14, 15, 16, 42, 78, 85, 154, 160, 161, 166, 177, 187, 196
masters, 77, 79, 80, 185
materials, xi, 6, 36, 78, 89, 103, 115, 116, 133, 144, 147, 159, 184, 204
media, 21, 26, 57, 72, 110, 147, 156, 173, 190
medical, 29, 105, 110, 122, 141
mental health, vi, xii, xiv, 21, 72, 75, 95, 96, 97, 98, 99, 100, 102, 103, 104, 105, 106, 107, 108, 109, 110, 122, 162, 163, 196, 204
micro-credential, xi, 78, 84, 85, 86, 87, 88, 89
modules, x, xiv, 56, 57, 62, 63, 64, 67, 86, 87, 113, 114, 126, 127, 146, 147, 162, 176, 183, 211
motivation, xii, 97, 98, 99, 103, 104, 123, 129, 146, 160, 161, 188, 190
multi-modal learning, 88

N

navigation, 85, 86, 92, 93
networking, 12, 60, 102

O

online education, v, x, xii, 13, 19, 24, 28, 77, 78, 85, 90, 91, 92, 102, 112, 113, 115, 119, 131, 132
online learning, ix, x, xi, 24, 25, 27, 28, 29, 30, 31, 36, 37, 39, 43, 44, 78, 85, 86, 92, 93, 95, 96, 97, 98, 106, 111, 112, 115, 136, 151, 160, 167, 176, 178, 181, 182, 185, 187, 189, 190, 203, 206
online learning and teaching, 112
online pedagogy, 203

online teaching, v, ix, xiii, 1, 2, 3, 6, 7, 8, 10, 11, 13, 14, 16, 18, 19, 36, 74, 83, 92, 132, 135, 147, 178

opportunities, vii, viii, ix, xiii, xiv, xvi, 3, 7, 11, 13, 15, 16, 30, 31, 37, 40, 43, 54, 85, 97, 98, 104, 111, 119, 155, 157, 161, 162, 166, 167, 175, 177, 182, 184, 188, 189

P

participation, 14, 19, 22, 25, 47, 71, 74, 83, 87, 152, 153, 156, 157, 159, 160, 161, 163, 164, 168, 172, 187, 188, 195, 204

participatory teaching, 81

pastoral care, 83, 90, 91

pedagogy, xvi, 26, 45, 72, 74, 152, 163, 182, 189, 203

peer support, x, 2, 5, 7, 15, 18, 19, 20, 21, 22, 52, 54, 55, 204, 206

personal contact, 55, 158, 198

personal life, 123, 124

personal problems, 160

personal relations, 123, 124

personal relationship, 123, 124

physical education, xii, 40, 112

physical environment, 40

physical health, xii, 112

platform, 9, 17, 32, 36, 38, 42, 180, 181, 185, 186

positive correlation, 3, 53, 59

principles, xi, 24, 28, 78, 85, 88, 116, 119, 120, 138, 181

professional development, 4, 8, 79, 85

professionals, xii, 41, 84, 85, 87, 112, 119, 120, 121, 122, 124, 125, 132, 184

project, 30, 31, 42, 54, 57, 155, 168, 190, 211

psychological distress, 109

psychological health, 96, 108, 119, 126

psychological processes, 49

public health, xiv, 125, 176, 193

public sector, 211

purposeful design, 78

Q

questioning, 135, 151, 155

questionnaire, 58, 59, 60, 61

quizzes, xi, 17, 73, 78, 88, 184

R

reading, 20, 33, 36, 91, 135, 148, 153, 156, 182

reality, 31, 41, 42, 93, 103, 178, 200, 203

recommendations, iv, xii, 2, 18, 44, 53, 61, 67, 96, 97, 103, 104

recovery, xvi, 5, 190, 193

researchers, 32, 79, 141, 202

resilience, xii, 96, 102, 108

resources, ix, xi, xii, 1, 6, 8, 9, 26, 31, 78, 80, 90, 93, 102, 105, 112, 114, 115, 116, 119, 125, 132, 136, 142, 147, 160, 168, 171, 182, 198, 200, 203

response, ix, xi, xii, xiv, 2, 5, 6, 16, 18, 27, 51, 54, 61, 77, 80, 81, 83, 84, 95, 96, 102, 113, 131, 158, 175, 198, 201

restrictions, xi, xii, 1, 2, 3, 16, 43, 77, 96, 98, 100, 101, 125, 130, 169, 198

risk, 15, 42, 91, 104, 121, 122, 137, 154, 158, 165, 166, 169, 201

S

school, xiii, 54, 57, 73, 97, 114, 137, 144, 168, 178

school learning, 114

schooling, 144

science, xi, 14, 47, 49, 69, 79, 84, 85, 89, 149, 150

scope, 156, 158, 202
self-assessment, 12
self-discovery, 145
self-efficacy, 47, 127, 129
self-monitoring, 129
self-paced, xi, 78, 84, 86, 91
self-paced learning, 79
self-reflection, 205
self-study, 142, 147
seminars, xiii, 133, 136, 143, 144, 145, 146, 147, 171, 198
semi-structured interviews, 195
services, iv, 4, 116, 206, 207, 210
social connectivity, 194
social construct, 24, 26, 27
social events, 104, 198
social interaction, x, 3, 25, 26, 27, 55, 68, 97, 99, 103, 200
social interactions, 26, 27, 55
social network, 105, 106, 186, 190
social support, 99, 101, 102, 103, 110
socialisation, 68, 96, 100, 102, 104
society, 29, 49, 82, 201, 207
solution, 5, 52, 55, 68, 104, 188, 203
stereotype, 158
stress, viii, 52, 56, 67, 74, 95, 96, 97, 99, 100, 101, 106, 109, 121, 122, 187
stressors, 97, 100, 102, 107, 108
structure, 8, 32, 36, 54, 78, 83, 85, 86, 98, 115, 161, 181
student engagement, vi, vii, viii, x, xiii, xiv, xv, xvi, 24, 30, 36, 39, 47, 51, 55, 56, 59, 67, 68, 70, 74, 75, 151, 152, 154, 156, 160, 162, 164, 165, 167, 168, 169, 170, 171, 172, 173, 175, 176, 179, 187, 188, 189, 190, 191, 205
student expectations, xiv, 194, 195, 196, 202, 208
student experience, vi, xiv, xv, 3, 7, 30, 38, 69, 74, 108, 153, 176, 179, 180, 186, 193, 194, 195, 199, 208, 211

student experience strategy, 208
student motivation, 52, 54, 56, 171
student populations, 44
student wellbeing, xii, xiv, 112, 117, 196, 203, 204
success, viii, x, xii, 22, 51, 55, 90, 111, 112, 113, 114, 115, 116, 117, 118, 119, 127, 133, 136, 139, 141, 143, 153, 161, 167, 177, 179, 180
support services, xiv, 57, 103, 196
survey based data, 194
symptoms, xii, 99, 100, 101, 107, 121, 124

T

teachers, 3, 20, 24, 25, 60, 81, 133, 134, 137, 138, 139, 140, 141, 142, 143, 144, 145, 146, 147, 170, 178, 182, 191
technical assistance, 4, 7, 16
technical support, 6, 115
techniques, ix, 30, 31, 126, 127, 128, 130, 137, 197
technological advances, 202
technologies, vii, ix, 2, 3, 6, 15, 16, 45, 135, 136, 156, 160, 172, 211
technology, viii, x, xiii, 2, 10, 11, 13, 14, 26, 27, 33, 44, 52, 54, 55, 56, 57, 68, 69, 90, 93, 104, 147, 152, 160, 161, 168, 196, 200, 203, 204, 206, 207, 209
tertiary education, 111, 119, 131
testing, ix, 11, 12, 13, 14, 15, 17, 18, 149
training, 11, 93, 124, 141, 143, 145, 147
transition, v, ix, x, xiv, 1, 2, 4, 14, 16, 18, 36, 52, 54, 56, 70, 71, 73, 78, 81, 93, 97, 98, 112, 114, 124, 170, 171, 175, 201, 203
trauma, 121, 122, 124

U

universities, vii, viii, ix, x, xi, 1, 2, 51, 68, 74, 80, 82, 89, 95, 96, 101, 103, 110, 134, 169, 172, 175, 176, 178, 194, 196, 197, 198, 199, 200, 201, 202, 204, 207, 208
university education, 97, 196, 201, 204

V

videos, 82, 88, 115, 116, 117, 128
virtual communities, 34
virtual fresher's fairs, 198

vocational training, 145

W

wellbeing, vi, xii, xiv, 95, 96, 97, 98, 99, 101, 102, 103, 104, 106, 111, 112, 113, 114, 115, 116, 117, 118, 119, 125, 126, 127, 128, 130, 131, 132, 160, 169, 196, 203, 204
workbook, 88, 115, 116
workload, 162, 167
workplace, 145
worldwide, vii, 51, 95, 96, 97, 100, 101, 178